Thomas Cook **pocket** guides

GENOA

Your travelling companion since 1873

Written by Pat Levy
Updated by Jan Fuscoe

Published by Thomas Cook Publishing
A division of Thomas Cook Tour Operations Limited
Company registration no. 3772199 England
The Thomas Cook Business Park, 9 Coningsby Road,
Peterborough PE3 8SB, United Kingdom
Email: books@thomascook.com, Tel: +44 (0) 1733 416477
www.thomascookpublishing.com

Produced by Cambridge Publishing Management Limited
Burr Elm Court, Main Street, Caldecote CB23 7NU
www.cambridgepm.co.uk

ISBN: 978-1-84848-406-1

© 2007, 2009 Thomas Cook Publishing
This third edition © 2011 Thomas Cook Publishing
Text © Thomas Cook Publishing
Maps © Thomas Cook Publishing/PCGraphics (UK) Limited
Transport map © Communicarta Limited

Series Editor: Karen Beaulah
Production/DTP: Steven Collins

Printed and bound in Spain by GraphyCems

Cover photography © Atlantide Phototravel/Corbis

CONTENTS

SYMBOLS KEY

The following symbols are used throughout this book:

ⓐ address   ☏ telephone   ⓦ website address   ⓔ email
🕒 opening times   Ⓝ public transport connections   ❶ important

The following symbols are used on the maps:

🄸 information office		■ point of interest	
✈ airport		O city	
➕ hospital		O large town	
🛡 police station		○ small town	
🚌 bus station		═ motorway	
🚆 railway station		─ main road	
Ⓜ metro		─ minor road	
✝ cathedral		─ railway	
❶ numbers denote featured cafés & restaurants			

Hotels and restaurants are graded by approximate price as follows:
£ budget price   **££** mid-range price   **£££** expensive

▶ *The Bigo provides stunning views of the city*

INTRODUCING
Genoa

Introduction

Genoa is one of Europe's big surprises. It sounds like just another Italian city with all that goes with it: museums, designer boutiques, pizza, mopeds – and it is all that – but it is also an unusual place with its own ideas about life and culture. On the surface, wandering around Porto Antico with its sights designed entirely for leisure and tourism, that proposition is a little hard to swallow, but walk 100 metres away from the Aquarium and you are in another world of tiny alleyways between looming medieval buildings, pathways winding upwards and away, crossing above your head, and ancient churches set in tangled piazzas. There is a maze-like quality to the place – you can never be quite sure that the alley you turn down isn't going to bring you right back to where you started from. The buildings, erected in the Middle Ages and rebuilt over the years, bombed in World War II and then picked up and put back together again in the following decades, are constantly changing. A renovation reveals Roman marble carvings or medieval columns, a rundown tenement becomes a bijou apartment block for the upwardly mobile, and a bookshop's shelves are built around what was once the nave of an ancient church.

The city's 'new' town has another identity, with the grand palaces of Via Garibaldi and wide, busy piazzas.

When the alleys and palaces get a little too much, you can visit the parks and gardens of Nervi, to the east, or take a comfortable train ride to the Italian Riviera, where you can loll on the stony beaches of Santa Margherita Ligure or trek the ancient pathways around the Cinque Terre to return refreshed and ready to explore some more of the ancient city.

🔺 Christopher Columbus stands proud in the Piazza Acquaverde

When to go

SEASONS & CLIMATE

Genoa is a good place to visit at any time of year, being blessed with a temperate maritime climate. The sea breezes usually stop the city getting too humid in summer and moderate the temperature in winter so that it rarely freezes. The tourist season gets going each year in spring – by May the temperature is typically around 20°C (68°F). Things hot up with average temperatures of 25°C (77°F) and low rainfall for the three months of summer. As in the rest of Italy, Genoa's residents tend to take their holidays in August. Families often head to the seaside, so the whole coastal region gets very busy.

Autumn begins in September and tends to carry on well into November. Lots of restaurants and other tourist-oriented places close between December and February. January is the coldest month, with temperatures averaging around 8°C, and with relatively high rainfall, although New Year celebrations in Porto Antico are still a highlight.

ANNUAL EVENTS

January
Celebrations of the New Year (31 Dec/1 Jan) in Porto Antico.

February
Fiera di Sant' Agata Held in the district of San Fruttuoso on the Sunday closest to Sant' Agata's memorial day (5 February). There are stalls of snacks and gifts.

Easter
Holy Week A series of processions in the week leading up
to Easter Monday. The most impressive is on the evening of
Holy Thursday.

April
Genoa Pesto World Championship An event held every two
years at the Palazzo Ducale to crown the maker of the best
pesto sauce. The next one will take place in 2012.

June
**Regatta delle Antiche Repubbliche Marinare (Boat Race of the
Maritime Republics)** Teams from Genoa, Pisa, Amalfi and Venice
compete in rowing races every fourth year at the start of the month.
Lots of processions and fun. The next regatta in Genoa is 2014.
Suq a Genova A ten-day, mid-month festival of multi-ethnic
cultures at Porto Antico. It has an exotic market, classes in ethnic
dance and cuisine, workshops for kids and, best of all, shows and
literary events.

● *Beach lovers are spoilt for choice along Liguria's coast*

Festival Internazionale di Poesia (Poetry Festival) Annual festival of the spoken word attracting the likes of Wole Soyinka, J.M. Coetzee and other artists from around the world. Held at the Palazzo Ducale. Ⓦ www.festivalpoesia.org

Eve of the Saint's Day of St John the Baptist Firework display in Porto Antico (23 June).

Feast of St John the Baptist Procession from San Lorenzo Cathedral to Porto Antico carrying the ashes of the saint and attended by the ancient Genoese fraternities (24 June).

July

Genoa Film Festival At Porto Antico and other venues.

Festivale Musicale del Mediterraneo Series of concerts and shows at Porto Antico, featuring traditional and popular music, plus a theatre festival held in Piazza San Matteo and a jazz improvisation festival at the end of the month (see page 12).

August & September

Procession dell'Assunta Evening procession on 15 August and firework display at Nervi.

Festa dell'Unità Porto Antico The last week in August and first week in September brings a festival held by the left-wing political parties. Music, concerts, theatre, children's entertainment and ballroom dancing, plus conferences and films.

September

La Notte Bianca The 'white night' is one of music and entertainment throughout Genoa (11 September).

October

Niccolò Paganini Prize Festival celebrating the life of Paganini, the highlight of which is a competition between talented young violinists, the winner getting the right to play the great man's violin.

Castagnata e Frisciolata alla Commenda In Piazza della Commenda in the last week of October, chestnuts and fried dumplings (*friscii*) are served to the public – all profits go to charity.

December

Circumnavigando Clown Festival Clowns fill the city, performing in piazzas and drawing passers-by into their performances. Circus tent in Porto Antico.

PUBLIC HOLIDAYS

Capodanno (New Year's Day) 1 Jan
La Befana (Epiphany) 6 Jan
Domenica di Pasqua (Easter Sunday) 25 Apr 2011; 8 Apr 2012; 31 Mar 2013
Lunedì di Pasqua (Easter Monday) 26 Apr 2011; 9 Apr 2012; 1 Apr 2013
Liberazione (Liberation Day) 25 Apr
Primo Maggio (Labour Day) 1 May
Festa della Repubblica (Republic Day) 2 June
Ferragosto (Feast of the Assumption) 15 Aug
Tutti Santi (All Saints' Day) 1 Nov
Festa dell'Immaculata (Feast of the Immaculate Conception) 8 Dec
Natale (Christmas Day) 25 Dec
Santo Stefano (Boxing Day) 26 Dec

Festivale Musicale del Mediterraneo

Among the many festivals celebrated in the city – jazz, religious festivals *et al* – the most recently inaugurated of them seems to be the one with the greatest impact. It began in 1992 as part of the celebrations of the 500th anniversary of the discovery of America by Genoa's favourite son, Christopher Columbus, and its organisers have travelled around the five continents ever since, looking for music to bring to the city. In its inaugural year it brought hundreds of musicians from around the world to the newly rebuilt Porto Antico. Performances were watched by thousands of citizens, and in the intervening years since its inauguration the festival has increased in size and scope.

Each year takes up a particular theme in music, and during Genoa's big celebratory year of 2004 (its year as Capital of Culture) the festival focused on the way music and dance from various traditions can find compromises and common themes. Performances mixed Hebrew and Arab music, flamenco and Pakistani music, and so on.

Performances centre on the great open space in Porto Antico, but do not stop there. The squares of the Old City are filled with musical performances throughout the day, and more conventional performances take place in the theatres around the city. There are also lots of accompanying workshops such as music therapy classes, masterclasses in musical technique and talks by leading musicians, and a series of performances aimed particularly at children, with animations, parades and shows. In 2008 many of the performances focused on the synthesis of music and images as live bands played along to films going back as far as Cecil B DeMille's 1915 version of *Carmen*. The festival is organised by **Associazione Echo Art** (🅐 Piazza delle Feste, Porto Antico 🅦 www.echoart.org) and tickets can be purchased from **fnac** (🅐 Via XX Settembre, 46r 🅣 010 290111).

🔺 *Joji Hirota & The Taiko Drummers perform at the Festivale Musicale*

History

Genoa's first appearance in the 7th century BC triggered a great deal of attention: various forces – Etruscans, Romans, Carthaginians, Goths, Byzantines, Arabs, Lombards and Saracens – attacked, destroyed, rebuilt and attacked it again. By the 11th century, a kind of relative stability was established. Genoa, now a city, was ruled by local families, who bickered and fought for power. The city began to dominate the region, built walls around itself to keep out invaders, and set up trading posts in the Levant. In the next century Genoa had its autonomy recognised by the Holy Roman Emperor and began some serious economic expansion.

By the 13th century it had a navy and a coinage, was in conflict with the other powerful seaports of Pisa and Venice and, by 1284, dominated trade in the Mediterranean. By the 14th century its power extended across Liguria. The 15th century saw the setting up of the first banks, the birth of Christopher Columbus and his trip to the Americas. In 1522 the city became a republic and a series of struggles began against the French, who wanted Genoa-owned Corsica for their own. Squabbling over Corsica continued for a couple of centuries and eventually, in 1768, Corsica became French.

In 1796 Napoleon took the city, and shortly afterwards the Austrians besieged it, during which time 30,000 Genoese starved to death. The next big event was the *Risorgimento*, the movement for Italian unity, in the early 19th century. In 1805 Giuseppe Mazzini, the leader of the movement, was born in Genoa. In 1860 Garibaldi came to Genoa, from where he began his campaign to free southern Italy from foreign domination. In 1861, Italian unity was complete and Genoa became one of many cities in the new state.

Things looked up for a while, with European aristocracy taking in the Ligurian coastline during their grand tours. *Palazzi* (palaces) were built, a railway line sprouted, large chunks of the city were remodelled on a bombastic scale and all went well until World War II. During this time, northern Italy was occupied by Germany and Genoa was heavily bombed by the Allies. After the war, rebuilding began, and Genoa became Italy's major seaport, with swathes of the western coastline given over to heavy industry and shipping. In recent decades Genoese industry has changed its nature from shipping and heavy industry to services; the old port, badly in decline, has been remodelled into a leisure area; the G8 summit was held here in 2001 (watched by the whole world as riots broke out in the streets), and lots of money was found for the 500th anniversary of Columbus' discovery of America and Genoa's role as European Capital of Culture in 2004. Certain events have shown how thoroughly elements of the city are steeped in Catholicism: the publication of *The Da Vinci Code* in 2005 saw Genoa become the focal point of protests against the book's criticism of the Church; two years later, one of the city's most powerful clerics, Archbishop Angelo Bagnasco, had to be put under armed guard when he spoke out against plans to give unmarried couples the same legal rights as married ones; and, finally, 2008 saw the much acclaimed visit of Pope Benedict XVI. On a more secular level, Genoa revealed its ambition to become Italy's greenest urban area when Mayor Marta Vincenzi announced his intention to create a sustainable development plan for the city.

Lifestyle

For most of the last century Genoa was a city dedicated to trade, heavy industry and shipping, despite its setting in the highly agricultural centre of Liguria. Its modern incarnation is different again, and as a result is a strange mix of country folk, shipyard workers and young, upwardly mobile service industry workers. It is a very young city, with a university that attracts students from all over Italy and beyond, and its homogeneous white Catholic society has seen an influx of refugees from Africa. The predominant lifestyle is hard-working and pleasure-loving. The older generations of families remember hardships and making do, and all Genoese love a good bargain. Ask anyone in Genoa which is the best restaurant and they'll send you to a long-established, inexpensive one.

The day starts early with a quick espresso and focaccia for breakfast, eaten either at home or standing up at one of the thousands of bars in the city. There's a long morning's work for the workers, while the home-maker spends his or her morning going from grocer to market stall to fish seller – supermarkets just haven't caught on here. Lunch is a long affair, in some cases businesses not reopening until 15.00, but the working day goes on longer to make up for it. In the evenings whole families go to their favourite restaurants or have long, chatty meals at home. Chairs are put out on the piazzas, and old men sit around watching the passers-by. The young often move straight from work to a bar and spend the early evening chatting with friends and filling up on the snacks that are often supplied with *aperitivi*, often not eating an evening meal at all. At weekends the family is out again, taking walks, having picnics and trying out the places to eat. By Sunday evening the city becomes a ghost town until Monday morning when a slow start is made, many shops not opening till the afternoon, as if the weekend was so much more their real life that it's hard to get going again.

◯ *The Genoese still prefer to shop the traditional way*

Culture

Genoa is very proud of its cultural roots. The city has a long tradition of music of all kinds, from opera and classical performances through to rock and jazz. Here, the opera and ballet are popular forms of art and the Genoese will tell you about the Genoa-born violinist and composer Paganini as easily as they will claim Christopher Columbus as one of their own. Opera in the city centres around the high-tech **Teatro Carlo Felice**, which, with its four stages, can put on that number of productions at any one time. A year-round programme of performances takes place here with as many as ten major productions in each year. The same theatre is the main venue for classical music, although there are other venues such as the Palazzo Ducale, where visiting performers play on Sundays. Ballet, too, is very popular, with a robust season of performances in the Carlo Felice, plus a ballet festival at Nervi in July. Genoa has a tradition of popular music known as *trallero*, which consists of five male singers with contrasting voices. Not so common in modern times, this form of singing was once popular in the bars of the Old City.

More conventional dramatic performances are chiefly to be found in the Teatro Carlo Felice, or in the grand 1,000-plus seater **Teatro della Corte**. Another theatre, **Teatro Gustavo Modena**, puts on performances of a more avant-garde nature, looking towards circus, fantasy or recitals and supporting new young writers. An old theatre in the city, **Teatro della Tosse**, is the home of the comedy writer Tonino Conte. Two more venues, The Duse Hall and Genovese Hall, offer programmes of musicals and comedy.

The Palazzo Ducale often hosts classical music performances

The annual Paganini competition (see page 11) is only part of a longer Paganini festival that celebrates the life of the composer and violin player. The events bring in musicians from as far away as Japan to play and compete for the prize of playing the master's violin.

The city's art galleries are worth coming to the city for, even if there was nothing else here. The fabulously wealthy merchants of the city collected art and much of it has remained here. The Palazzo Rosso is the gallery to head for first, but there are many more galleries as well as churches with their own art treasures. The buildings themselves are also a strong part of the culture of the city. The Renaissance *palazzi* are as important as the art collections inside them, and the modern offerings of Renzo Piano – the Porto Antico, the Sphere and the Bigo – all add to the cultural importance of the city.

▶ *The medieval archway of the Porta Soprana*

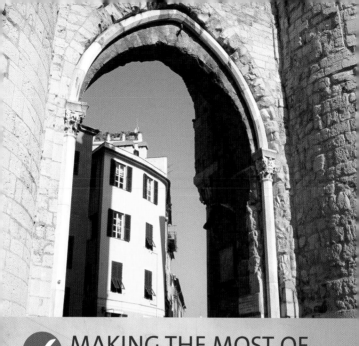

 # MAKING THE MOST OF
Genoa

Shopping

Shopping isn't the first thing you think of when making a trip to Genoa, but for the truly dedicated there are plenty of reasons for planning that extra space in the carry-on luggage. The city certainly provides lots of opportunities for clothes shopping. Via Roma is where all the zeros are to be found on price tags, with D&G, Ferragamo, Louis Vuitton and the other usual suspects taking pride of window space. Coming down a few zeros, the next port of call is **Via XX Settembre**, where there are some lovely clothes in very Italian styles both in chain stores and small, one-off boutiques.

If you are looking for gifts for your friends back home and mementos for your mantelpiece then head out of town, where each village has its own hand-thrown pots and peculiar handicrafts, some of which attractively capture the crazy forms of the streets and houses of the district.

SHOPPING ETIQUETTE

Genoa really hasn't adopted the grab-it-and-run style of British shopping, and most shops are quite tiny and personal places, run by their owners who often sit making their products on the premises. In Genoa, as in the rest of Italy, it is customary to greet the shopkeeper when you go into a shop and attempt to explain what you are looking for. They will show you what they have and you can choose to buy or not. As you leave, another round of salutations takes place. Quite civilised really.

Food is a definite possibility if you are thinking of bringing something home. Olive oil from the area is a worthwhile investment, and deli shops also do interesting lines in prepared sauces: *pesto alla Genovese* is excellent to bring home, as is *sugo di noce* (walnut sauce), very typical of Ligurian cooking. *Pandolce* (fruit loaf) is sold in every bread, focaccia and cake shop in town. Shop-made sweets are worth seeking out. Pietro Romanengo at Via Soziglia 74 makes and sells all manner of sweet things and packages them up just as it has been doing

◆ *Genoa's main shopping street, Via XX Settembre*

USEFUL SHOPPING PHRASES

What time do the shops open/close?
A che ora aprono/chiudono i negozi?
Ah keh awra ahprawnaw/kewdawnaw ee nehgotsee?

How much is this?
Quant'è?
Kwahnteh?

Can I try this on?
Posso provarlo?
Pawssaw prawvarrlaw?

My size is ...
La mia taglia è ...
Lah meeyah tahlyah eh ...

I'll take this one, thank you
Prenderò questo, grazie
Prehndehroh kwestaw, grahtsyeh

Can you show me the one in the window/this one?
Può mostrarmi quello in vetrina/questo?
Pooh oh mawstrahrmee kwehllaw een vehtreenah/kwehstaw?

This is too large/too small/too expensive
Questo è troppo grande/troppo piccolo/troppo caro
Kwestaw eh tropaw grahndeh/tropaw peekawlaw/trawpaw kahraw

for generations. It's important to note that many shops close during the entire month of August when many Genoese take their holidays. This doesn't apply to department and chain stores.

Eating & drinking

If you are used to the multi-ethnic cuisines of most big cities, Genoa might come as a bit of a shock. Lots of Genoese restaurants proudly include the word *antica* (old) in their name. New is definitely not necessarily good in Genoa, although innovative styles are starting to make tiny inroads. That said, it doesn't mean that you're in for a dull time. Fish, fruit and vegetables predominate, and although pork, rabbit, beef and chicken are represented, it would be hard not to come here and spend some of your meals eating fresh greens or seafood.

Most Genoese menus have four courses. *Antipasti* is usually a tiny course, often seafood but also sliced cured meats or tiny savoury pies or pastries. The next course is pasta such as *trenette*, flat strips, or *trofie*, curls served with a sauce. Alternatively, for this course, especially in winter, you could try *mesciua*, a soup made from beans, chickpeas and pieces of spelt, or Genoese minestrone, with lots of vegetables, pasta and pesto. Main

PRICE CATEGORIES

The price ratings here are based on a four-course meal for one person without wine.

£ up to €20   **££** €20–55   **£££** over €55

In cheaper restaurants you should leave about five per cent of the bill as a tip, and in pricier restaurants, around ten per cent, unless the bill states that a service charge has been added.

🔺 *Stock up for a picnic with some delicious local treats*

courses are based around meat, often rabbit or fish, and served with plainly cooked vegetables or a piece of focaccia.

Look out for traditional desserts such as *pandolce*, a teeth-breaking biscuit stuffed with dried fruits, or *baci*, little pies made from nuts, eggs and chocolate.

Other staples are nuts. Chestnut trees are planted all over the city and feature in many classic dishes. At Christmas they are ground into flour for pancakes and, at other times, help to make a kind of *tagliatelle* and even a bread called *la pattona*. Walnuts feature in pasta courses as a sauce over a kind of ravioli called *pansôti*, which is filled with vegetables. The classic sauce of Genoa is, of course, pesto. Legend has it that Frank Sinatra had his pesto shipped in to Hollywood from one restaurant in Genoa.

Instead of pizza, try some of the produce of the local pie shops. One of these is *farinata*, a dough made from chickpea flour, olive oil and water, and eaten hot. Another is *torta di riso*, an enormous pie made from layers of thin rice pastry covering spinach mixed up with flour, eggs and creamy *quagliata* cheese. *Focaccia alla Genovese*, a yeasted flatbread filled with herbs and occasionally cheese, is ubiquitous and very tasty.

Genoa is as obsessed, as are other Italian cities, with *aperitivi*, which are served in bars from around 19.00 and come with a quantity of nibbles: *crostini*, mini pizza or perhaps pieces of ham or cheese. Many people don't bother with dinner – they find their favourite *aperitivi* place and munch on snacks all night.

Picnicking in the city is almost as much fun as eating out – the focaccia places sell supremely tasty, ready-made delights to carry off to a green spot, and there are delicatessens selling all kinds of cured meats and cheeses to accompany bread from the bakeries.

USEFUL DINING PHRASES

I would like a table for ... people
Vorrei un tavolo per ... persone
Vawrray oon tahvawlaw perr ... perrsawneh

Waiter/waitress!
Cameriere/cameriera!
Cahmehryereh/
cahmehryera!

May I have the bill, please?
Posso avere il conto, per favore?
Posso awehre il cawntaw,
perr fahvawreh?

Could I have it well cooked/medium/rare please?
Potrei averlo ben cotto/mediamente cotto/poco cotto
per favore?
Pawtray ahvehrlaw behn cawtaw/mehdeeyahmehnteh
cawtaw/pawcaw cawtaw perr fahvawreh?

I am a vegetarian. Does this contain meat?
Sono vegetariano/vegetariana (fem.). Contiene carne?
Sawnaw vejetahreeahnaw/vejetahreeahnah.
Contyehneh kahrneh?

The Genoa area is famous for a wine made in the Cinque Terre
called *sciacchetrà*, made from grapes that are left to dry in the sun
before fermenting, producing a very strong sweet wine. Other
local wines to look for are Vermentino and Pigato, dry white wines,
and Rossese di Dolceaqua, from the Ligurian region.

Entertainment & nightlife

Genoa isn't really a tourist city. It still essentially belongs to its citizens, and the evening is often when you will see them out and enjoying themselves. The Old City is filled with tiny bars and cafés with tables set out in every available *piazzetta* or even just in the road. Here, depending on the style of the place, is where the Genoese entertain themselves. The bars are where the best *aperitivi* can be found, where there is often a live musician or two at weekends, where you can watch independent films projected up on to the walls of the bar and where all the local gossip gets aired.

Clubs and discos don't really exist in Genoa. There are a number of bars by the port where the locals hang out after a day on the beach and many stay open until around 01.00 or 02.00 during the summer months. Those looking for an elegant clubbing experience should head to **Il Covo** in Santa Margherita (see page 114).

There are often open-air music performances in the squares in summer. In the **Cinque Terre** there is an ongoing series of performances of all kinds organised by the regional authority. These take place in local churches or halls and range from string quartets to local folk and Latin American music. In Monterosso, the local squares are often the venue for live music organised by the bars and restaurants. In Genoa, classical concerts are held in churches throughout the city as well as at the Palazzo Ducale at weekends. Check with the tourist office for listings. The weekend Palazzo Ducale concerts can be booked at their box office (☎ 010 588866).

◆ Teatro Carlo Felice with Garibaldi in the foreground

Opera is a big hit in Genoa. **Teatro Carlo Felice** (see page 79) blasts taped opera into the square for most of the day and is a sight in itself. Its year-round programme is very popular. The somewhat expensive tickets can be booked at ⓦ www.carlofelice.it. The theatre is also the city's best venue for ballet.

Theatre runs all year in the city, but there is a theatre season during the winter when productions in Italian take place. Contact the tourist office to check what's on. Tickets for the theatre and other performances at the city can be bought online at ⓦ www.ticketone.it

There are cinema complexes located around the city and most of them have one day a week when films are shown in their original language. One, **Multi-Sala Ariston** (ⓐ Vico San Matteo ⓣ 010 2473549), has a daily English-language programme. Listings can be checked at ⓦ www.cinema-online.net. Regular cinema showings are always dubbed rather than subtitled. In summer, films are shown in the city's parks, but these are most likely to be in Italian.

There isn't much available in the way of English-language listings magazines except for a free multilingual booklet that is available in most hotel receptions. The tourist offices are your best bet and are really helpful, with plenty of leaflets to hand out and some good maps of the city.

Sport & relaxation

Bikes
There are lots of suitable roads for mountain biking in the
Ligurian region and the city recently introduced a cycle scheme.
The **Touring Club Italiano** can be found in the Palazzo Ducale
and provides maps and information. For cycling around the city,
on an electric or pedal bike, **MoBike** has cycle stations all over
the city. ❶ 800 132995

Boat tours
Consorzio Liguria Viamare Boat trips of the harbour depart daily
all year, and trips to Portofino, Santa Margherita Ligure and the
Cinque Terre from June to September. Pickup is at Calata Zingari
and beside the Aquarium. ⓐ Via Sottoripa 7/8 ❶ 010 265712
Ⓦ www.liguriaviamare.it

Diving
Arco 89 Diving and sailing services ⓐ Calata di Mari
❶ 010 255720 Ⓦ www.arco89.it
Polo Sub Diving Centre ⓐ Magazzini del Cotone Mod 2
❶ 010 2475252 Ⓦ www.polosub.it
San Fruttuoso Diving Centre ⓐ Via Favale 31, Santa Margherita
Ligure ❶ 0185 289574 Ⓦ www.san-fruttuoso.it

Football
Both Genoa CFC and Sampdoria play at the Stadio Luigi Ferraris.
Tickets can be booked at the addresses below.

Genoa a Via Garibaldi 3 t 010 612831 w www.genoacfc.it
Sampdoria a Piazza Borgo Pila, 39–5A, Torre B t 010 5316711
w www.sampdoria.it

Hiking

There are hundreds of kilometres of footpaths throughout the
region. In particular the Cinque Terre has some excellent walks,
as does the area around Portofino. For helpful maps and
information about the walks try:
Turismo in Liguria a Via Roma 11 t 010 576791
w www.turismoinliguria.it

⬥ *A boat trip along the Ligurian coast is a highlight*

Parco Naturale Regionale di Portofino ⓐ Via le Rainusso 1, Santa
Margherita Ligure ⓣ 0185 289479 ⓦ www.parks.it

**Ufficio di Informazione e di Accoglienza Turistica
(Tourist Information & Hospitality Office)**
Manarolo ⓣ 0187 760511
Monterosso ⓣ 0187 817059 ⓦ www.parks.it
Riomaggiore ⓣ 0187 762187
Vernazza ⓣ 0187 812533

Paragliding
Albatross Parapendio Ass. ⓐ Sportiva di Volo da Diporto,
Via Bobbio 282r ⓣ 010 8398710

Sightseeing Tours
A hop-on, hop-off bus visiting all parts of the city leaves from
Piazza Caricamento. ⓦ www.turismo.comune.genova.it

Whale-watching
Whale Watch Liguria departs from the Aquarium (see page 74)
at 13.00 on Saturdays between April and October and
additionally on Tuesdays from July to August. It should be noted
that the literature shows a picture of a dolphin, so don't be
disappointed if you don't get whales. On board is a WWF
biologist. There are reductions for children under 14, and under
3-year-olds go free. Advance booking. ⓣ 010 265712
ⓦ www.whalewatchliguria.it

Accommodation

The chief form of accommodation in Genoa is the series of star-rated hotels (*alberghi*) in the city. B&Bs are a new concept here, but there are a few of them around, while the other options are rooms to rent (*camere*) and campsites (*campings*). A 5-star rating generally implies quite a high degree of luxury (there is a 5-star-plus rating) including room service, multilingual staff and more, while from 3-star upwards, bathrooms are en-suite, alarm calls and telephones are in the rooms, and there are lifts, heating (air conditioning is 4- & 5-star only) and daily housekeeping (4- and 5-star is twice daily). Below 3-star you may find reception is unmanned for part of the day so doors are locked, en-suite bathrooms are extra, and there may only be a lift after the first floor.

The peak times for tourist-oriented hotel bookings in the city are during the summer months as well as during the annual boat show in the long, warm autumn. Lowest room rates are available from November to February. Strangely, the more expensive hotels, which are targeted at business travellers, tend to be cheaper during the summer months and at their most expensive in the autumn.

PRICE CATEGORIES
Hotel, guesthouse, B&B and hostel ratings are based on the average price of a double room in high season including breakfast.
£ up to €100   **££** €100–200   **£££** over €200

Areas in which to find budget accommodation in the city include the Old City, the area around Via Balbi and around Stazione Brignole. Some of the budget hotels around the Old City are situated in some very dark, narrow alleyways and those of a nervous disposition might like to avoid these, although there is very little danger – except that you may encounter some exotically dressed sex workers.

Out of the city at Santa Margherita Ligure, and especially at Portofino, rates are higher than in the city. In the Cinque Terre booking accommodation ahead can be problematic, since few places have websites and most are quite small and fill up quickly. The tourist office in Monterosso has a free leaflet and map listing all the hotels and rooms for rent in the village. Riomaggiore has a few options (see page 122) that can be booked online.

HOTELS

Acquaverde £ Well buffed-up 2-star hotel: good value for money at €50–100 for an en-suite room with TV, air conditioning and room safe. Plus it's right on nicely lit Via Balbi, has its own restaurant and takes credit cards. ❸ Via Balbi 28–29 (The Old City) ❶ 010 265427 Ⓦ www.hotelacquaverde.it

Hotel Major £ This 1-star place just off Via Luccoli is very central, has en-suite rooms with TV for under €70 including breakfast, a bar and friendly, English-speaking staff. Its location down a side alley is a bit offputting. ❸ Vico Spada 4 (The Old City) ❶ 010 2474174 Ⓦ www.hotelmajorgenova.it

⬥ *Understated luxury at the Grand Hotel Savoia*

Astoria ££ This 3-star place gives visitors such a relaxing stay that it's almost a little holiday all on its own. It's an ancient hotel that was renovated delicately enough to avoid destroying the late 19th-century design. The lift is an antique (and quite a time capsule), with a seat inside and gates you have to pull shut, and the rooms are big and air-conditioned, with all the usual amenities. Excellent self-service breakfast. ⓐ Piazza Brignole 4 (The Old City) ⓣ 010 873316 ⓦ www.hotelastoria-ge.com

Bentley ££–£££ The city's second 5-star hotel opened in 2007 and is a luxurious option for those looking for a stylish room, top facilities and a reasonably central location. ⓐ Via Corsica 4 ⓣ 010 5315111 ⓦ www.bentley.thi-hotels.com

Grand Hotel Savoia ££–£££ Located just next to the Principe Station, the GHS is 5-star luxury. Renovated in 2008, the rooms are stylish and comfortable, facilities are excellent and the views from the restaurant terrace are fabulous. Try the outdoor whirlpools on the roof. ⓐ Via Arsenale di Terra 5 (Via Balbi & around) ⓣ 010 27721 ⓦ www.grandhotelsavoiagenoa.com

Locanda di Palazzo Cicala ££–£££ The Locanda is a very stylish, modern place and, happily, it's also very central, with huge rooms set in an ancient *palazzo*. To up the luxury even more, each of these rooms is individually designed, and all have quite exquisite bathrooms. The rather enchanting common areas overlook Piazza San Lorenzo. Some rooms sleep three or more, which is convenient if you're travelling mob-handed. ⓐ Piazza San Lorenzo 16 (The Old City) ⓣ 010 2518824 ⓦ www.palazzocicala.it

Best Western Hotel City £££ A 4-star luxurious hotel whose considerable charms simmer seductively in a quiet location close to Piazza dei Ferrari. ⓐ Via San Sebastiano 6 (The Old City) ⓣ 010 586301 ⓦ www.bestwestern.it or ⓦ www.jollyhotels.it

HOSTEL

Hostel Genova £ The very reasonable price (from €17) is for a room in a dorm in Righi. Private rooms are available, too. Open Feb–Dec. ⓐ Via Giovanni Constanzi 120 ⓣ 010 2422457 ⓦ www.ostellogenova.it

CAMPSITE

Villa Doria £ On the road to Pegli to the west of the airport. This is a big park with around 200 pitches, open all year. ⓐ Via al Campeggio Villa Doria 15 ⓣ 010 6969600 ⓦ www.camping.it/english/liguria/villadoria

THE BEST OF GENOA

This compelling city has a great deal to offer and, however short your stay, you will find yourself entranced. If that were not enough, the beautiful Ligurian coastline is one of Europe's best-kept secrets.

TOP 10 ATTRACTIONS

- **The Aquarium** Spend a day getting up to some decidedly fishy business with these magnificent creatures (see page 74).

- **Palazzo Rosso** Take a perch alongside the culture vultures at this banquet of art (see page 85).

- **Bigo** Wobble upwards over the harbour, hold that camera steady and get an unforgettable eyeful of the city (see page 58).

- **Cattedrale di San Lorenzo (San Lorenzo Cathedral)** Wonder in awe at the sheer magnificence of this great church whose regular makeovers have allowed it to age beautifully (see page 62).

- **Boat tour** Take a boat to Portofino, stopping off at San Fruttuoso on the way (see page 104).

- **Walking tour** A wander through the characterful, narrow alleyways of the Old City will tell you everything you need to know about the place and its people (see page 58).

- **Railway adventure** For an absolutely peak experience, take a trip high into the mountains on the Genova-Casella railway (see page 81).

- **Meal in Zeffirino** Enjoy classic Ligurian cuisine in the city's most famous restaurant: if it was good enough for Frank (Sinatra) and Luciano (Pavarotti), it might be good enough to tempt you (see page 73).

- **Window-shopping** Wander around the *caruggi*, admiring the expensive designer boutiques interspersed with little artisan shops (see page 85).

- **A trip on the funicular** A ride on the funicular is a phenomenon in itself, and it will take you all the way to the city's fortifications (see page 94).

🔻 *The Chiostro di Sant'Andrea*

Suggested itineraries

HALF-DAY: GENOA IN A HURRY

In half a day you can race down Via Garibaldi and take in one or two of the museums, have lunch in Trattoria da Maria (see page 86), the most authentic and best-value restaurant in town, and check out **Cattedrale di San Lorenzo (San Lorenzo Cathedral)**. Take a quick stroll around the Porto Antico and a trip on the Bigo and you'll have caught much of the feel of this intriguing city.

1 DAY: TIME TO SEE A LITTLE MORE

In a day, besides Via Garibaldi and its museums, there is time perhaps for a quick sortie into the medieval heart of the city, where Roman marble, medieval brickwork and 21st-century pastiche are all jumbled together, providing shelter for African food stores, tiny boutiques, cafés and bars and ancient forgotten churches. Enjoy some Ligurian cuisine for dinner, then wander along to **Piazza delle Erbe** for wine or coffee and good company.

◆ *Enjoy breathtaking views of the city*

2–3 DAYS: TIME TO SEE MUCH MORE

With two or three days you can really get to know the city. Consider arranging a personal guided tour of the Old City through the tourist board. You must take a boat tour of the harbour – it is a truly impressive trip. Porto Antico, the **Aquarium** and the **Sphere** are well worth a half day. Go to the Galata Museum café for *aperitivi* one evening. Shop along **Via XX Settembre** to see why Italians always look so well dressed. Collect some eatables from one of the many *focaccerie* or delis and seek out hidden gardens for a reflective lunch. Take a bus ride out eastwards to the parks and seaside towns of Nervi and Boccadasse.

LONGER: ENJOYING GENOA TO THE FULL

A one- or two-day trip out to the Cinque Terre, visiting each of the pretty seaside villages and doing some of the walks between them, makes you realise that this is still one of the really unspoilt parts of western Europe. An overnight stay in Monterosso or Riomaggiore after the crowds have gone home is like a trip into the early 20th century – another culture emerges. Spend a day in Santa Margherita Ligure and take the bus ride around hairpin bends to Portofino and go celeb-spotting. A trip to the mountain village of Casella or one of the stops along the route on a narrow-gauge train, crossing chasms on ancient brick viaducts and finding simple local trattorias for lunch, is another highlight of a longer stay in the city. Your nights can be a crawl around the bars of Piazza delle Erbe and the surrounding streets, or find an outside table along Via San Lorenzo and people-watch over a meal.

Something for nothing

Genoa is a city where most of the fun is to be had just wandering around its narrow ancient streets. Every turn brings some new antiquity or curiosity, a bar or a shop to wonder at. Try window-shopping along **Via XX Settembre** and exploring the Mercato Orientale (Eastern Market) for the things you never thought it possible to eat. Take a cheap bus ride to Nervi or Boccadasse and have a wander around. The Cimiterio di Staglieno (Staglieno Cemetery) is filled with statues, and it can be interesting to look for the tombs of the famous.

Find your way into the **University Department of Architecture**, where you can discover the pretty roof garden and climb to the top of the building for fine views over the harbour. Walk up to Castello d'Albertis and sit in its gardens surveying the industrial landscape to the west of the city. Take an evening stroll around the Porto Antico admiring the space and design of the area, and watch the bats flying around the struts of the Bigo. These are the sorts of experience that are priceless, and not solely because they're available at no price! If you don't mind looking a bit of a nitwit, or if you have children who you can pretend begged you to take them on it, you can take the free ride around the city in the electric car shaped like a big white train, hopping on and off at the various sights. For some free – and unforgettable – culture, pop into the *palazzi* along **Via Garibaldi** to look at the paintings and rococo decorations (though it's always a good idea to ask the concierge first). If you like opera you can find a bench or a café outside the **Teatro Carlo Felice** and listen to the music.

◆ *Enjoy the tranquillity of Genoa's historic* palazzi

When it rains

Clearly the museums and churches of the city come into their own on a rainy day. The **Aquarium** has to be the best place of all, especially if you have children. It is filled with strange habitats and tanks where you can handle the creatures. Right outside is **La Sfera** (the Sphere), a large greenhouse of tropical plants and creatures, where you can pretend for half an hour or so that it's sunny and hot, and lined up in the shopping arcade next door are *gelaterie* and cafés. The museums of **Via Garibaldi** are along one stretch of road and can easily take up half a day of waiting for the rain to stop.

Shopping is still a pleasant experience in the rain, as long as you do it in **Via XX Settembre**, which has porticos along both sides of the street for much of its length. The covered footpaths are dotted here and there with well-protected cafés to take the strain out of retail. An interesting sight along this street is the Mercato Orientale (Eastern market), where all manner of produce is on sale, including fruit and vegetables, cheeses, flowers and more. The second floor houses more, including a bead shop and some clothes and shoe stalls.

If you are into your third or so day of rain then (a) you've really chosen a bad time to visit and (b) it may be the right day to see an English-language film. Fortunately lots of the cinemas show films in their original language at least one day a week. Alternatively, you could make this the day that you try out opera for size – the theatre is high-tech and very impressive, and the experience is worth having even if the opera is sung in another language and you have no idea what they are singing about.

🔺 *Bask in the tropical heat of the Sphere*

On arrival

TIME DIFFERENCE
Genoa is one hour ahead of GMT. Clocks go forward one hour on the last Sunday in March and back one hour on the last Sunday in October.

ARRIVING
By air
Cristoforo Colombo Airport (📞 010 60151 🌐 www.airport.genova.it) is 6 km (3¾ miles) west of the city. The airport is linked with the city by a bus service (called Volabus). Tickets costing €6 are available from the machine beside the bus stop, or the driver will sell you one. The ticket must be validated in the machine when you board. Journey time to the city is around 20 minutes but the Volabus ticket is valid for one hour, so make the most of it. City buses run from 05.30–23.45. Please note that unlike Volabus tickets, these can be used on other buses for 24 hours after purchase. The airport has a post office, several car-hire places, a newsagent, a tourist office and a café in the arrivals area. In the departures area a single coffee stall is the only opportunity to buy refreshments besides the duty-free shop.

By rail
Genoa has two main train stations linked with one another, **Stazione Principe** and **Stazione Brignole** (📞 199 166177 🌐 www.trenitalia.it). Stazione Principe has a tourist office. From Stazione Principe it is a brief walk to most of the tourist hotels or to Porto Antico, while from Stazione Brignole, buses 14,

17, 18, 19 and 33 go to Piazza dei Ferrari. Flat-rate bus tickets (€1.20, valid for 90 minutes) to anywhere in the city can be purchased at the kiosks outside the two stations or from newsagents. A carnet of ten tickets costs €11. They must be validated in the machine on the bus. Taxis wait outside the two stations and are metered. There is a flat rate of €7 per person (min. 3 people) to Principe Station and €8 (per person) to Brignole.

By road

Genoa is linked by motorway-class routes to most major cities in Italy and to the UK through the Swiss Alps or via the French Riviera. The journey time from the UK is 24 hours or more, including breaks. Cars are banned from the medieval centre of the city, and even in other parts of the city moving about is difficult. If you choose to drive to Genoa you might consider finding a hotel on the outskirts of the city and leaving your car there when you come in. A further consideration before opting to arrive in the city by car is

🔺 *A quick bus journey links airport and city*

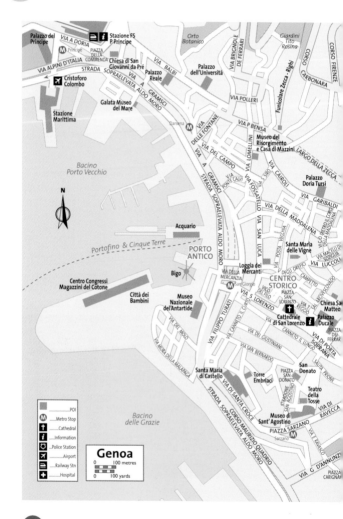

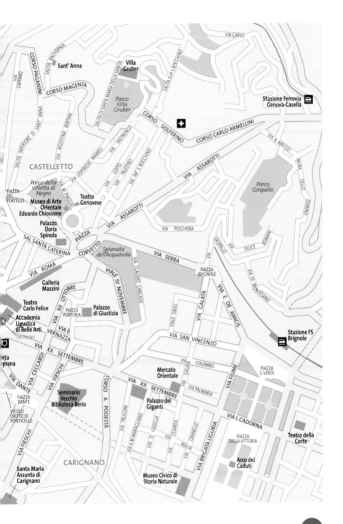

that traffic is heavy on the routes along the coast in summer. Roads off the main routes are narrow and tortuous, petrol stations scarce and closed on Sundays and parking is highly restricted in the resorts. Cars are banned in the Cinque Terre.

FINDING YOUR FEET

Number one on the list of things to do to acclimatise if you are British is to remember to look left first when crossing the road. In addition, it is important to recognise that pedestrian crossings have different rules to those used in Britain. Motorists are not required to stop at crossings for pedestrians. In the city this isn't

IF YOU GET LOST, TRY ...

Excuse me, do you speak English?
Mi scusi, parla inglese?
Mee scoozee, parrla eenglehzeh?

Excuse me, is this the right way to the old town/the city centre/the tourist office/the station/the bus station?
Mi scusi, è questa la strada per città vecchia/al centro città/l'ufficio informazioni turistiche/alla stazione ferroviaria/alla stazione degli autobus?
Mee scoozee, eh kwehstah lah strahda perr lah cheetta vehkyah/ahl chentraw cheetteh/looffeechiaw eenforrmahtsyawnee tooreesteekeh/ahlla stahtsyawneh ferrawvyarya/ahlla stahtsyawneh delee aowtoboos?

so much of a problem because traffic moves so slowly, but outside of the city do be aware of this. If you step out, speeding cars will usually stop but they won't stop for you if you stand politely at the kerb. A third traffic problem to be aware of is that even if a green man is showing, cars can turn off a main road into the side road that you are using. Apart from that, Genoa is an easy city to settle into once you have a map of the *caruggi*, the narrow alleyways of the Old City. Maps can be picked up at your hotel or the tourist offices. It is probable that you will get lost, so avoid making your first trip late at night when most of the shops are closed up and street lights few and far between. Genoa has its share of muggers, although it isn't a particularly dangerous city to wander around late at night. Keep wallets, purses and cameras out of sight and wear shoulder bags across your chest.

ORIENTATION

Genoa consists of a long, built-up strip following the port and coastline. As soon as you leave the streets immediately behind the port you are heading upwards, so if you get lost always head downhill, which will bring you back to the port. It is quite compact as a city and most sights can be reached on foot.

The tourist heart of the city is bounded by Via Balbi, which runs into town from Stazione Principe, Via Garibaldi along the north, and Via Roma and Via Dante, which form the eastern boundary. In between these streets is the most confusing warren of alleyways you will ever encounter and it is *de rigueur* for you to get lost on your first sortie inside. The major landmark here is Piazza dei Ferrari, a huge square with a fountain at its centre and through which many of the city's buses run. From the Piazza,

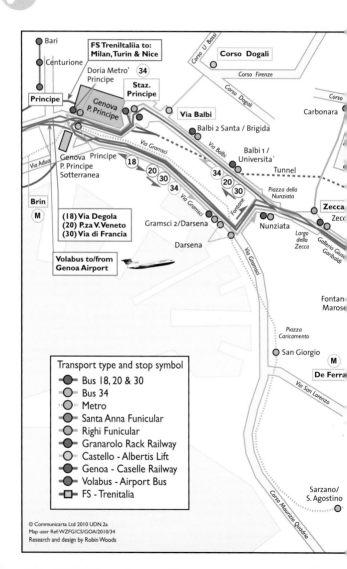

Bari

Centurione

Principe

Doria Metro'
Principe

**FS Treniltaliia to:
Milan, Turin & Nice**

(34)

**Staz.
Principe**

Genova
P. Principe

Genova
P. Principe
Sotterranea

Principe

Via Adua

Brin

(M)

(18)

(20)

(30)

(34)

**(18) Via Degola
(20) P.za V. Veneto
(30) Via di Francia**

**Volabus to/from
Genoa Airport**

Via Gramsci

Corso U. Bassi

Corso Dogali

Corso Firenze

Corso Dogali

Corso

Carbonara

Via Balbi

Balbi 2 Santa / Brigida

Via Balbi

Balbi 1 /
Universita`

Tunnel

Piazza della
Nunziata

Zecca

Zecc

(34)

(20)

(30)

Fontane

Gramsci 2/Darsena

Darsena

Nunziata

Largo
della
Zecca

Galleria Giuse
Garibaldi

Via Gramsci

Fontan
Marose

Piazza
Caricamento

San Giorgio

(M)

De Ferra

Via San Lorenzo

Corso Maurizio Quadrio

Sarzano/
S. Agostino

Transport type and stop symbol

- Bus 18, 20 & 30
- Bus 34
- Metro
- Santa Anna Funicular
- Righi Funicular
- Granarolo Rack Railway
- Castello - Albertis Lift
- Genoa - Caselle Railway
- Volabus - Airport Bus
- FS - Trenitalia

© Communicarta Ltd 2010 UDN.2a
Map user Ref:WZFG/CS/GOA/2010/34
Research and design by Robin Woods

Bus 35
→ Via Vannucci → CORSICA/
MENTANA

ON ARRIVAL ✓

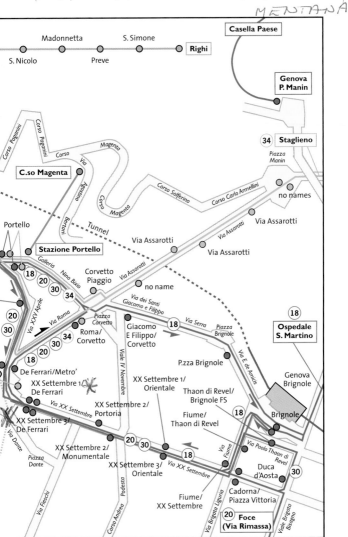

Casella Paese

S. Nicolo   Madonnetta   S. Simone
         Preve   Righi

Casella Paese

Genova
P. Manin

34 Staglieno

Piazza
Manin

Corso Paganini
Corso Paganini
Corso
Magenta
Via Agostino

C.so Magenta

Corso Solferino   Corso Carlo Armellini

no names

Via Assarotti

Corso Magenta
Bertoni

Tunnel

Via Assarotti

Via Assarotti
Via Assarotti

Portello

Galleria
Nino Bixio

Stazione Portello

18
20
30
34

Corvetto
Piaggio

no name

Via dei Santi
Giacomo e Filippo

18   Via Serra

Piazza
Brignole

18   Ospedale
     S. Martino

20
30

Via XXV Aprile
Via Roma

Piazza
Corvetto
Roma/
Corvetto

Giacomo
E Filippo/
Corvetto

18

20
30
34

Via E. de Amicis

Genova
Brignole

18

De Ferrari/Metro'
XX Settembre 1/
De Ferrari

Viale IV Novembre

P.zza Brignole

Brignole

XX Settembre 1/
Orientale

XX Settembre 2/
Portoria

Thaon di Revel/
Brignole FS

18

Via XX Settembre

Fiume/
Thaon di Revel

Via Paola Thaon di Revel

XX Settembre 3/
De Ferrari

Via Dante

Piazza
Dante

XX Settembre 2/
Monumentale

20
30

Via Fieschi

Corso Andrea Podesta

XX Settembre 2/
Orientale

XX Settembre 3/
Orientale

Via XX Settembre

18

Via Fiume

Duca
d'Aosta

30

Fiume/
XX Settembre

Cadorna/
Piazza Vittoria

Via Brigata Liguria

20   Foce
     (Via Rimassa)

Viale Brigata Bisagno

Via XX Settembre runs eastwards and is the city's major shopping area; it brings you close to Stazione Brignole which, for most tourists, is as far east within the city as they will travel.

GETTING AROUND

Most people find that by far the best way of getting about the city is on foot. City buses charge a flat rate of €1.20 (valid for 90 minutes) and tickets can be bought at newsstands and *tabacchi*. In addition to the buses, a funicular railway travels from Largo della Zecca to Righi in the suburbs. In Piazza del Portello another funicular travels to Castelletto. Again, flat-rate tickets can be bought at newsstands and validated on board the transport. There is also a metro system which runs from Piazza dei Ferrari down to Porto Antico and along the waterfront to Certosa. The system is currently being extended as part of a long-term plan to take it further west of the city.

CAR HIRE

Car hire in Italy is expensive. The international companies have desks in the airport and you should arrange the hire before arriving in Genoa, especially in July and August.

Avis Cristoforo Colombo Airport ☎ 010 6515101 Ⓦ www.avis.com

Europcar Cristoforo Colombo Airport ☎ 010 6504881 Ⓦ www.europcar.com

Hertz Cristoforo Colombo Airport ☎ 010 6511191 Ⓦ www.hertz.com

Maggiore Cristoforo Colombo Airport ☎ 010 6512467 Ⓦ www.maggiore.it

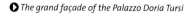

▶ *The grand façade of the Palazzo Doria Tursi*

THE CITY OF
Genoa

The Old City

This area includes the ancient heart of the city and all its main streets leading higgledy-piggledy down to the Porto Antico, which is now regenerated as a tourist hub. If you are going to get lost in Genoa it will be here, but lost here means good fun – or a map will help you get back to the harbour. This area of the city is awash with lovely shops, both along Via XX Settembre and in the labyrinth of tiny streets that make up the old part of the city. To the east are the weekend-tripper villages of Nervi and Boccadasse.

SIGHTS & ATTRACTIONS

Bigo

Designed by the Italian architect Renzo Piano to look like the masts of a sailing ship, this is a revolving lift that hoists its occupants up 40 m (130 ft) above the port, providing panoramic views of the harbour, as well as the hills behind the city and tiny matchstick people wandering about below. The trip takes less than ten minutes. ⓐ Porto Antico ⓣ 010 2485711 ⓦ www.portoantico.it ⓛ 10.00–20.00 Tues, Wed & Sun, 10.00–23.00 Thur–Sat, closed Mon ⓘ Admission charge

Casa di Colombo (Columbus' house)

Genoa's claim on the man who 'discovered' America is that as a child he lived in one of the houses in the street that used to be here. In 1992, in preparation for the celebrations for the anniversary of the discovery, this house was saved and renovated

◯ *Columbus' house, so they say*

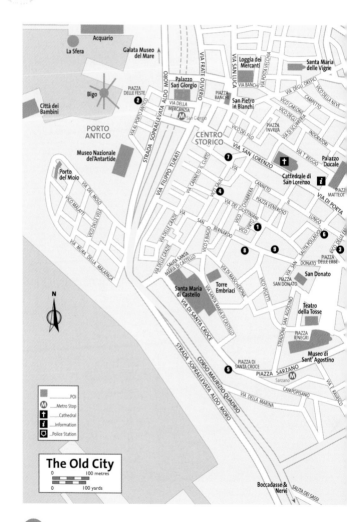

Acquario

La Sfera

Galata Museo del Mare

Bigo

Città dei Bambini

PORTO ANTICO

Museo Nazionale dell'Antartide

Porto del Molo

VIA DEL PORTO ANTICO

STRADA SOPRAELEVATA ALDO MORO

VIA FRATE OLIVERIO

PIAZZA DELLE FESTE

VIA SAN LUCA

Loggia dei Mercanti

Santa Maria delle Vigne

Palazzo San Giorgio

VIA BANCHI

San Pietro in Bianchi

PIAZZA BANCHI

VIA DELLA MERCANZIA

San Cosmo

VIA DELLA POSTA VECCHIA

VIA DEGLI ORELICI

VICO DELLA NEVE

CAMPETTO

VICO CARLONE

VICO DEL GIUSTIANI

VIA DI SCURREIA

INDORATORI

PIAZZA INVREA

VICO DEL FIO

CENTRO STORICO

VIA SAN LORENZO

Cattedrale di San Lorenzo

Palazzo Ducale

PIAZZA MATTEOT

VIA FILIPPO TURATI

VIA CANNETO IL CURTO

VIA DELLE GRAZIE

VICO MALATTI

VICO DELLE VELE

VIA DEL MOLO

VIA MURA DELLA MALAPAGA

VIA DEI GIUSTINIANI

PIAZZA VENEROSO

CANNETO IL

VIA DI PORTA

LUNGO

VIA SAN BERNARDO

VICO S.BIAGIO

SANTA MARIA DI CASTELLO

VIA DI MASCHERONA

VIA DI SANTA CROCE

Santa Maria di Castello

Torre Embriaci

VIA SANTA MARIA DI CASTELLO

SANTA MOLIARDI

VIA SAN DONATO

PIAZZA DELLE ERBE

VICO DELLE

PIAZZA SAN DONATO

San Donato

PIAZZA SARZANO

VIA VEGETTI

Teatro della Tosse

STRADONE SAN AGOSTINO

PIAZZA R.NEGRI

Museo di Sant'Agostino

CORSO MAURIZIO QUADRIO

STRADA SOPRAELEVATA ALDO MORO

PIAZZA DI SANTA CROCE

PIAZZA SARZANO

Sarzano

VIA DELLA MARINA

CAMPOPISANO

VIA E.RASSCO

SALITA DEI SASSI

Boccadasse & Nervi

N

The Old City

0 _____ 100 metres

0 _____ 100 yards

POI

Metro Stop

Cathedral

Information

Police Station

VIA CORSICA 4

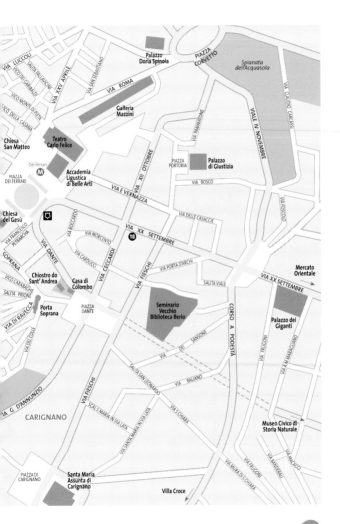

as possibly being his childhood home. Next door is a pretty ruin – the Chiostro do Sant' Andrea (cloister of St Andrew). ⓐ Vicolo Dritto Di Ponticello, off Via Dante ⓣ 010 2516714 ⓛ 09.00–12.00, 14.00–18.00 daily ⓘ Admission charge

Cattedrale di San Lorenzo (San Lorenzo Cathedral)

Founded in the 9th century, done over in Romanesque style in the 12th century and then given a Gothic facelift in the 13th, the cathedral also has 15th- and 17th-century bits added on. The medieval doors tell stories from the Bible and the martyrdom of St Lawrence, one of the city's patron saints. Highlights are the Cappella di San Giovanni Battista and the Museo del Tesoro, which holds booty from the Crusades, and the silver chest said to contain the ashes of St John, which is carried around the city on 24 June. ⓐ Piazza San Lorenzo, off Via San Lorenzo ⓣ 010 2471831 ⓛ 09.00–12.00, 15.00–18.00 Mon–Sat, closed Sun ⓘ Admission charge for museum

Chiesa del Gesù (Church of Jesus)

Quite modern by the standards of most churches in Genoa, this one was begun in 1589, and among its elaborate Baroque interior decorations are two paintings by Peter Paul Rubens, which are well worth seeking out. ⓐ Via Francesco Petrarcha 1 ⓣ 010 2514122 ⓛ 10.30–12.00, 16.00–19.00 daily

Palazzo San Giorgio

Built in the 12th century and extended in the 16th, the building has been at times a bank, a prison (Marco Polo did some time here) and the centre of government. The frescoes on the western

⬤ *Chiesa del Gesù hides some artwork gems on the inside*

façade were rediscovered during renovations in the 1990s, and are the work of Lazzaro Tavarone. You can go inside to admire the 16th-century statues of the city's movers and shakers and an enormous hearth dating from 1554. Exhibitions are occasionally held here. ⓐ Via della Mercanzia ❶ 010 2412625 ❶ Check for opening hours with the tourist office

Porta Soprana

Two battlemented towers form an archway, which is part of the 11th-century fortifications of the city. You can go up into one of the towers at weekends and admire the view. ⓐ Via di Ravecca 47 ❶ 010 2465346 ❶ 09.00–12.00, 14.00–18.00 Sat, Sun & public holidays, closed weekdays

Porto Antico

This big open space is filled with cafés, a museum, cinemas, the Bigo, the museum of the Antarctic and the ice-skating rink, all put together by Italian architect Renzo Piano. Wandering around, you will notice Porto del Molo, another of the city gates, built in 1553. ⓐ Museo Nazionale del'Antartide ❶ 010 2543690 ⓦ www.mna.it ❶ 10.30–18.30 daily ❶ Admission charge

San Donato

Hidden deep in the *caruggi* is this 11th-century parish church, a fascinating amalgam of recycled stonework – the marble carvings over the doorway and possibly some of the internal pillars are Roman in origin, while the façade is largely 19th century. Inside are some worthy artworks, including a Madonna of the Graces by the 15th-century painter Niccolò da Voltri.

ⓐ Piazza San Donato 35r ☏ 010 2468869 🕒 08.00–12.00, 15.00–17.00 daily

Santa Maria di Castello

If you haven't had your fill of ancient churches yet, visit this grand edifice, begun in 1549. The grand staircase leading up to

EXCURSIONS FROM THE OLD CITY

The tiny fishing village of **Boccadasse**, a suburb to the east of the Old City, is well worth a trip on the bus for a stroll round the picturesque, gaily painted houses stacked up on the hills beyond the harbour. If you like a quiet time, avoid Sundays, when the Genoese all seem to head east for a stroll along the Corso Italia to Boccadasse.

Nervi, a seaside town further along the east coast, is another playground of the city where the Genoese go out for their evening stroll. The highlight is the 2-km (1¼-mile) stroll along the Passeggiata Anita Garibaldi, with great views of the coastline. Also here are four museums: the Galleria di Arte Moderna, the **Mitchell Wolfson Jr Collection** (ⓐ Villa Saluzzo Serra, Via Capolungo 3 ☏ 010 3726025 🌐 www.gamgenova.it 🕒 10.00–19.00 Tues–Sun, closed Mon), Raccolte Frugone and Museo Luxoro. The gardens of the adjoining villas have been converted into an 9-hectare (22-acre) public park.

Both Boccadasse and Nervi can be reached by bus from Via Dante. 🚌 Bus: 42 (Boccadasse) 15, 17 (Nervi)

the church is 19th century, while much of the statuary in the façade is 18th century. Inside the work is largely 16th and 17th century, with some notable paintings by Domenico Fiasella and Guercino. ⓐ Piazza di Caragnano ⓣ 010 540650 ⓛ 07.30–11.30, 16.00–18.30 daily

CULTURE

Museo Civico di Storia Naturale (Natural History Museum)

Ancient elephant skeletons, 19th-century collectors' zoological finds and stuffed animals in glass cases. ⓐ Via Brigata Liguria 9 ⓣ 010 564567 ⓦ www.museidigenova.it ⓛ 09.00–19.00 Tues–Fri, 10.00–19.00 Sat & Sun, closed Mon ⓘ Admission charge

Museo di Sant' Agostino

Reconstructed as an auditorium, the 13th-century church is worth peeking into, but the real draw here is the museum built into

---

VILLA CROCE

A brief bus ride away, Villa Croce is home to the **Museo di Arte Contemporanea** (Contemporary Art Museum) and boasts over 3,000 pieces of modern art by Ligurian and international artists. The gallery is set in pretty gardens overlooking the sea and hosts regular exhibitions. ⓐ Via Jacopo Ruffini 3 ⓣ 010 580069 ⓦ www.museovillacroce.it ⓛ 09.00–19.00 Tues–Fri, 10.00–19.00 Sat & Sun, closed Mon ⓝ Bus: 12, 15 from Stazione Brignole, 35 from Stazione Principe ⓘ Admission charge. Free on Sundays

the adjoining monastery and cloisters. It contains sculptures collected from the ruins of destroyed churches. The highlight is the funeral monument of Margaret of Brabant by Giovanni Pisano, her face showing expression and the folds of her clothing showing quite natural movement, rare in the Middle Ages. ⓐ Piazza Sarzano 35r ⓣ 010 2511263 ⓦ www.museidigenova.it ⓛ 09.00–19.00 Tues–Fri, 10.00–18.30 Sat & Sun, closed Mon ⓘ Admission charge

RETAIL THERAPY

Antica Drogheria M Torelli Very long-established shop selling herbal remedies, soap, perfumes and more. ⓐ Via San Bernardo 32r ⓣ 010 2468359 ⓛ 09.00–18.30 Thur–Tues, 09.00–12.30 Wed

Blu Antica Gabriella Pasini sits quietly in this shop, throwing and painting beautiful blue pots. ⓐ Via della Maddalena 34–6r, off Via San Luca ⓣ 010 2461239 ⓛ 09.00–19.00 Mon–Sat, closed Sun

La Casa Ligure Very touristy shop selling Ligurian products, but they're so nice you're bound to pick up something. Artwork, food, sweets, wine. ⓐ Via di Ravecca 11/13r ⓣ 010 2462601 ⓦ www.lacasaligure.it ⓛ 09.00–19.00 Mon–Sat, closed Sun

Feltrinelli Bookshop with fairly extensive collection of thrillers and classics in English, maps, guides etc. ⓐ Via XX Settembre 233r ⓣ 010 540830 ⓛ 09.30–20.00 Mon–Sat, 10.00–13.00, 16.00–20.00 Sun & public holidays

⬤ *Mushrooms and much more at the Mercato Orientale*

Mercato Orientale The city's biggest fresh produce market where you can buy huge smoked hams, porcini mushrooms and fresh chestnuts, horsemeat if you fancy it, lovely cheeses, imported fruit, fresh fish and tasty bread. ⓐ Via XX Settembre ⓛ 05.00–21.00 daily

Serafina Delicatessen selling all you'd ever need for the city picnic as well as dried *funghi*, preserved vegetables, and lovely things in jars, trays of oil and bottles. ⓐ Via Canneto il Curto 34 ⓣ 010 2468779 ⓛ 08.15–13.00, 16.00–19.30 Mon–Sat, closed Sun

Standa This is the place to pick up all the stuff you forgot to bring (or the airline wouldn't let you carry on board). Italian supermarket with an excellent range of food. ⓐ Via Cesarea 12r, off Via XX Setembre ⓛ 08.00–20.00 Mon–Sat, 09.00–13.00, 15.30–19.30 Sun

L'Ultima Volta che Vidi Parigi With a name as long as that, there must be something here to look at. Very classy clothes at very nearly affordable prices. Buy something here to remind you of how beautifully the Italians can dress. ⓐ Via XX Settembre 123r ⓣ 010 5954500 ⓛ 09.30–19.30 Mon–Sat, closed Sun

TAKING A BREAK

Antica Trattoria Sà Pesta £ ❶ Great pies made from rice flour and local soft cheese – plus whatever they found in the market that morning – go into the huge wood-fired oven to be turned into mouthwatering peasant food. Pizzas and focaccia, plus many different pies, can be bought to take out or eat in the spick-and-span little dining room. Lovely. ⓐ Via dei Giustiniani 16r ⓣ 010 2468336 ⓛ 10.00–22.00 Mon–Sat, closed Sun

Bigo Café £ ❷ Right outside the Bigo so you can watch the thing go up and down. Spacious café bar, blackboard with the day's menu outside, simple lunch dishes, pizzas, ice cream. Food served till midnight and open late. ⓐ Via al Porto Antico ⓣ 010 2470587 ⓛ 08.00–02.00 daily

La Cremeria delle Erbe £ ❸ Reputed to be the best *gelateria* in Genoa, this place is located in the city's coolest square and stays open till 02.00 at weekends. More flavours than you ever imagined possible. ⓐ Vico delle Erbe 15–17r ⓣ 010 2469254 ⓛ 11.00–01.00 daily (02.00 Fri & Sat)

Da Da £ ❹ This bookshop, design centre and café lurks quietly among the ancient buildings of the medieval quarter. Nice combination of wine, books and food. ⓐ Via dei Giustiniani 3r ⓣ 010 2541530 ⓛ 12.00–21.00 Mon–Sat, closed Sun

La Passeggiata Librocaffè £ ❺ Spacious bookshop-cum-café set in the remains of an ancient church. Standard menu includes some very un-Ligurian fare from crêpes to waffles. Beer and wine and some good coffee. ⓐ Piazza di Santa Croce 21r ⓣ 010 2543644 ⓦ www.plogp.com ⓛ 08.00–23.00 Mon–Sat, closed Sun

Caffè degli Specchi ££ ❻ Named after the mirrors that line the ground floor (and which are preserved from the original bar that stood here), this is an enormously popular place, serving coffee and breakfast and an excellent lunch. Long, white cocktail bar downstairs, ancient panelled dining room upstairs. ⓐ Salita Pollaiuoli 43r ☎ 010 2468193 🕒 08.00–15.00 daily

AFTER DARK

RESTAURANTS

Borobudur ££ ❼ One of the city's few ethnic restaurants, this place offers spicy Indonesian food adapted to Italian tastes and divided into several region-oriented four- or five-course meals. Quiet Balinese music accompanied by Balinese dancing and that gentle Balinese welcome. ⓐ Via Canneto il Lungo 8r ☎ 010 2475310 ⓦ www.borobudur.it 🕒 12.00–14.00, 19.00–24.00 Thur–Tues, closed Wed

Le Colonne di San Bernardo £££ ❽ Lovely setting for this restaurant – the 16th-century Palazzo Giustiniani. Come here to eat and enjoy the surroundings or spend the evening just down the road in their outdoor seating area sampling the wine and watching the passers-by. ⓐ Via San Bernardo 59r ☎ 010 2461252 🕒 18.00–01.30 Tues–Sun, closed Mon

Pintori £££ ❾ Sardinian cooking in this long-established restaurant deep in the heart of the Old City. Popular at lunchtime. The Sardinian menu is translated for English-speakers and ranges from suckling pig through Sardinian versions of pasta – try sweet ravioli made with honey – to more recognisable fish dishes. ⓐ Via San Bernardo 68r ☎ 010 2757507 🕒 12.30–14.30, 19.30–22.30 Mon–Fri, closed Sat & Sun

● *Try the fine Ligurian seafood dishes at Zeffirino*

Zeffirino £££ ⑩ The most famous restaurant in the city has been here since the 1930s, seeing out the Allied bombing of World War II. Sinatra and Pavarotti have eaten here. Very Ligurian cuisine. ⓐ Via XX Settembre 20 ⓣ 010 5705939 ⓦ www.ristorantezeffirino.it ⓛ 12.00–24.00 daily

BARS & CLUBS
Banano Tsunami Situated just beneath Bigo (see page 58) with views of Genoa as well as out to the sea, this bar is open late and fills up with all those looking for good cocktails and nibbles along with some fresh sea air. ⓐ Piazza delle Feste, Porto Antico ⓛ 12.00–01.00 daily

Bar Berto Loud, busy bar in Piazza delle Erbe, this one with a large menu of pizzas, focaccia and more substantial dishes. Most of the action is outside at the tables, but there is some seating inside if you don't mind the loud music. ⓐ Piazza delle Erbe 6r ⓣ 010 2758157 ⓛ 11.00–02.00 daily

Taggiôu A wine bar in the middle of the *caruggi* serving fine wines along with plates of cured meats and cheeses. ⓐ Vico Superior del Ferro 8 ⓣ 010 2759225 ⓛ 12.00–15.00 & 19.00–23.00 Mon–Sat, closed Sun

Threegaio Another lively bar in Piazza delle Erbe serving *aperitivi*, snacks during the day and some good cocktails. ⓐ Piazza delle Erbe 17–19r ⓣ 010 2465793 ⓛ 10.00–02.00 Mon–Thur, 10.00–03.00 Fri & Sat, 18.00–02.00 Sun

Via Garibaldi & around

This area of the city contains examples of what are known as
Le Strade Nuove – new streets. The title has now perhaps become
misleading as they actually date from the 16th and 17th centuries.
The most well known of these is Via Garibaldi, which is lined with
palazzi – grand houses built in individual styles by the oligarchy
that ruled Genoa in the 16th century. At this time the Old City
had become highly constricted and there was no room for Genoa's
nouveau riche to express their confidence in their wealth. Also in
this area are Via Roma and Via XXV Aprile, full of designer shops, and
Piazza dei Ferrari, that rather grand statement of Genoese pride.

SIGHTS & ATTRACTIONS

Acquario (Aquarium)

The enormously popular Aquarium (over a million visitors every
year) is built into a ship moored in the Ponte Spinola. Among the
exhibits are a hummingbird forest, penguins and sharks.
Children will love the touch pool where they can bond with
skate, stingrays and other fish. ⓐ Ponte Spinola ❶ 010 2345678
ⓦ www.acquariodigenova.it ❶ 09.30–19.30 Mon–Fri,
09.30–20.30 Sat, Sun & public holidays ❶ Admission charge

Cimitero di Staglieno (Staglieno cemetery)

Filled with some stunning statuary as well as the graves of
many famous Genoese. Woodlands make the cemetery into a
pleasant rural area. Look out for the tomb of the political leader
Giuseppe Mazzini, the statue of *Faith* by Santo Varni and the

⬤ *The elegant, traffic-free Via Garibaldi*

THE CITY

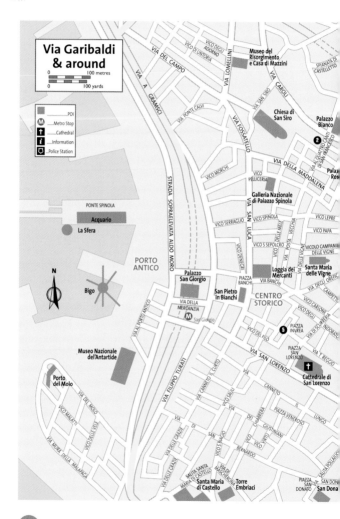

Via Garibaldi & around

0 — 100 metres
0 — 100 yards

- ■ ....POI
- Ⓜ ....Metro Stop
- ✝ ....Cathedral
- ⓘ ....Information
- Ⓟ ....Police Station

VICO DEGLI ADORNO
VICO DI UNTORIA
VIA DEL CAMPO
VIA LOMELLINI
Museo del Risorgimento e Casa di Mazzini
SPIANATA DI CASTELLETTO
VIA A GRAMSCI
VIA CAROLI
VIA PONTE CALVI
VIA SAN SIRO
Chiesa di San Siro
Palazzo Bianco
VIA FOSSATELLO
VIA QUATTRO CANTI DI SAN FRANCESCO
❷
VIA DELLA MADDALENA
Palaz Ros
VICO MORCHI
VICO PELLICERIA
Galleria Nazionale di Palazzo Spinola
VICO LEPRE
STRADA SOPRAELEVATA ALDO MORO
PONTE SPINOLA
Acquario
La Sfera
VICO SERRAGLIO
VIA SAN LUCA
VICO SPINOLA
VICO DELLE VIGNE
VICO VECCHIA
VICO LEPRE
VICO PAPA
VICOLO CAMPANILE DELLE VIGNE
VICO S SEPOLCRO
VIA POSTA VECCHIA
Santa Maria delle Vigne
N
PORTO ANTICO
Bigo
Palazzo San Giorgio
VICO VENEZIA
PIAZZA BANCHI
Loggia dei Mercanti
VIA BANCHI
VIA DEGLI OREFICI
VIA DELLA MERCANZIA
San Pietro in Bianchi
CENTRO STORICO
VICO CARLONE
VICO DEGLI INDORATU
Ⓜ San Giorgio
VIA AL PORTO ANTICO
VICO DEL FILO
❺
PIAZZA INVREA
VIA T REGGIO
VIA DI SOZZIFERA
Museo Nazionale del'Antartide
PIAZZA SAN LORENZO
VIA SAN LORENZO
✝
Cattedrale di San Lorenzo
Porto del Molo
VIA FILIPPO TURATI
VIA CANNETO IL CURTO
VICO SAULI
IL CANNETO
PIAZZA VENEROSO
LUNGO
VICO MALUATI
VIA DEL MOLO
VIA DELLE VELE
VIA DI CHIABRERA
VICO VIRTÙ
GIUSTINIANI
PIAZZA SAN DONATO
VIA MURA DELLA MALAPAGA
VIA DELLE GRAZIE
VIA DI SAN BERNARDO
VICO S BIAGIO
VIA DI MASCHERONE
SCURIA SULIVALI
SAN DON
SANTA SANTA MARIA DI CASTELLO
Santa Maria di Castello
Torre Embriaci
San Dona

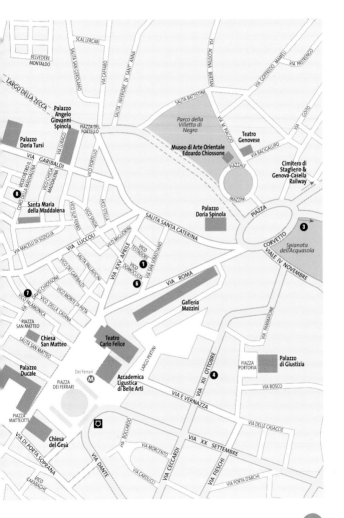

SCAL LERCARI

BELVEDERE
MONTALDO

VIA SAN GEROLAMO

VIA CAFFARO

VIA AGOSTINO BERTANI

VIA INFERIORE DI SANT' ANNA

VIA GOFFREDO MAMELI

VIA PASTERNGO

LARGO DELLA ZECCA

Palazzo
Angelo
Giovanni
Spinola

PIAZZA DEL
PORTIELLO

SALITA BATTISTINE

Parco della
Villetta di
Negro

SALITA INFERIORE DI SANT' ANNA

VIA M.PIACCIO

Teatro
Genovese

VIA COLO

VIA BACIGALUPO

Palazzo
Doria Tursi

VIA TURSI

VIA GARIBALDI

VIA CHIESA MADDALENA

VICO PORTIELLO

VICO DIETRO IL CORO DELLA MADDALENA

Museo di Arte Orientale
Edoardo Chiossone

PIAZZALE

Cimitero di
Staglieno &
Genova-Casella
Railway

❽ Santa Maria
della Maddalena

VICO SUP FERRO

VICO STELLA

MAZZINI

PIAZZA

VIA MACELLI DI SOZIGLIA

VIA LUCCOLI

SALITA PALERMINI

VICO DEI GARIBALDI

SALITA SANTA CATERINA

Palazzo
Doria Spinola

CORVETTO

❸

VIA XXV APRILE

VICO MIGLIORINI

VICO TESTADORO

VICO SAN SEBASTIANO

❶

Spianata
dell'Acquasola

VIALE IV NOVEMBRE

❼ VICO PALAMONICA

VICO CHIOSSONE

VICO MONTE DI PIETÀ

VICO DOMOCULTA

❻

VIA ROMA

PIAZZA
SAN MATTEO

VICO DELLA CASANA

Galleria
Mazzini

SALITA SAN MATTEO

Chiesa
San Matteo

Teatro
Carlo Felice

VIA PAMMATONE

Palazzo
Ducale

Dei Ferrari Ⓜ

LARGO PERTINI

VIA XII OTTOBRE

❹

PIAZZA
PORTORIA

Palazzo
di Giustizia

PIAZZA
DEI FERRARI

Accademica
Ligustica
di Belle Arti

VIA E. VERNAZZA

VIA BOSCO

PIAZZA
MATTEOTTI

🏛

VIA DELLE CASACCIE

Chiesa
del Gesú

VIA DI PORTA SOPRANA

VIA DANTE

VIA XX SETTEMBRE

VICO CARBAGHE

VIA BOCCARDO

VIA MORCENTO

VIA CECCARDI

VIA CARDUCCI

VIA FIESCHI

VIA PORTA D'ARCHI

PETER PAUL RUBENS AND WORLD WAR II

Although Rubens, a Flemish painter, seems to have spent little time in Genoa, which he visited in the early 17th century, he was so taken by the new houses he saw in Le Strade Nuove dei Palazzi (as Via Garibaldi was called when it was first built) that he made very detailed architectural drawings of them. These drawings were referred to after the bombings of World War II to assist in the reconstruction of those that had been most badly damaged.

Cappella dei Suffragi. ⓐ Piazzale Resasco 1 ☎ 010 870184
🕐 07.30–17.00 daily, closed public holidays Ⓝ Bus: 12, 14, 34, 48

Palazzo Doria Tursi

One of the grand palaces of Via Garibaldi, built in 1569 for Niccolò Grimaldi, and currently government offices. Several of the rooms are open to the public. There's a lovely interior courtyard surrounded by pink and white stonework, and a grand staircase. A museum inside includes one of Niccolò Paganini's violins, and three letters signed by Christopher Columbus.
ⓐ Via Garibaldi 9 ☎ 010 2758098 Ⓦ www.museidigenova.it
🕐 09.00–19.00 Tues–Fri, 10.00–19.00 Sat & Sun, closed Mon

Piazza Banchi & Loggia dei Mercanti

Piazza Banchi was once the commercial heart of the city, connecting the businesses of the old town with the harbour. Typical of many *loggias* (open galleries) throughout the city, Loggia dei Mercanti was originally built for the city's moneychangers. In the 16th century it became, for a time, the city's stock exchange. The roofed pathway around the buildings was glassed-in during the 19th century and the courtyard is now home to a few market stalls selling flowers, CDs and books. San Pietro in Banchi was built in the 16th century with shops underneath, the rent from the shops financing the building of the church, and God and Mammon finding a common bottom line. ⓐ Piazza Banchi

Piazza dei Ferrari & Teatro Carlo Felice (Carlo Felice Opera House)

Piazza dei Ferrari was created in the 19th century to ease traffic problems. The fountain, designed by Giuseppe Crosa, arrived in the 1930s, and the modern theatre, which you can visit, was rebuilt almost entirely in 1992 after its destruction in World War II. The pedestrianised area was constructed in 2001. The piazza is a major hub where buses coming into the city disgorge city workers, and is not a particularly relaxed place, but it is home to the Palazzo Ducale, Teatro Carlo Felice (the opera house) and Chiesa del Gesù (Church of Jesus). ⓐ Piazza dei Ferrari ⓘ Opera house: 010 5381224 ⓦ www.carlofelice.it ⓛ Tours on Mon by appointment

Piazza San Matteo

This fascinating, pretty square, bounded on one side by Chiesa San Matteo, was once the headquarters of the powerful Doria clan, numbering thousands, who ruled this part of the city. They once owned all the buildings here, and the piazza could be barricaded in times of infighting between the clans. The buildings contain *loggia* which would once have had the traders' goods laid out. The church was the clan's private place of worship and has a pretty cloister garden. Several Dorias are buried in the crypt. ❶ 010 2474361 ◐ Chiesa San Matteo: 09.00–12.00, 15.00–18.00 daily

◬ *The Piazza dei Ferrari is the city's busy hub*

GENOVA–CASELLA RAILWAY

From Via alla Stazione per Casella it is possible to take a ride on the narrow-gauge railway to Casella, 24 km (15 miles) from Genoa. The 55-minute journey passes through some stunning scenery, taking in three valleys en route. All the stations are starting points for walking routes through the area and there are lots of bike-hire outlets and restaurants. The train ride is very popular at weekends. ⓐ Via alla Stazione per Casella 15 ⓣ 010 837321 ⓦ www.ferroviagenovacasella.it ⓘ Book in advance

Santa Maria delle Vigne

This area of the city was dominated by the Grillo family, who commissioned the rebuilding of the 10th-century church in 1640. All that remains of the earlier version is the bell tower. The highly ornate interior is covered in gilding and contains 17th-century frescoes. The façade dates back to 1842. ⓐ Vicolo Campanile delle Vigne 5 ⓣ 010 2474761 ⓦ www.irolli.it ⓛ 08.00–12.00, 15.00–19.00 daily

La Sfera (The Sphere)

Designed by Renzo Piano, this is basically a large greenhouse containing lots of tropical plants, insects and lizards. It stands beside the Acquario on Ponte Spinola, alongside the lines of moored tour boats that cruise the harbour and visit the villages to the east. ⓐ Ponte Spinola ⓛ 10.00–19.00 daily (Mar–Oct); 10.00–17.00 daily (Nov–Feb) ⓘ Admission charge

CULTURE

Accademia Ligustica di Belle Arti (School of Fine Arts)

Set in a 19th-century *palazzo*, this museum of art contains
works by Ligurian artists from the 16th to 19th centuries.
ⓐ Largo Pertini 4 ① 010 581957 ⓦ www.accademialigustica.it
🕒 09.45–17.30 Tues–Fri, 10.00–18.00 Sat & Sun, closed Mon

Galleria Nazionale di Palazzo Spinola

The Spinolas were another one of the city's ancient families to
donate their palace and art collection to the state (one begins
to suspect that some of them had tax issues). The building itself
is an impressive sight with some surviving frescoes dating back
to the house's earlier owners, the Grimaldi family, and two
floors of the house hold a collection of Italian and Flemish
Renaissance art that includes works by Giovanni Pisano and
Rubens. ⓐ Piazza Pelliceria 1, off Vico Pelliceria ① 010 2705300
ⓦ www.palazzospinola.it 🕒 08.30–19.30 Tues–Sat, 13.30–19.30
Sun, closed Mon ❗ Admission charge

Museo di Arte Orientale Edoardo Chiossone
(Edoardo Chiossone Museum of Oriental Art)

Housed in the Parco Villetta di Negro, this collection of oriental
art was donated to the city by the 19th-century painter
whose name graces the museum's title. The huge collection,
containing some very rare pieces, includes paintings, armour,
weapons, ceramics and woodcarvings. ⓐ Piazzale Mazzini 4
① 010 542285 ⓦ www.museidigenova.it 🕒 09.00–19.00
Tues–Fri, 10.00–19.00 Sat & Sun, closed Mon & public holidays

🚌 Bus: 34, 37 from Stazione Principe, 18 from Stazione Brignole
ⓘ Admission charge

Palazzo Bianco

European, Italian and Genoese paintings from the 17th to 19th centuries. In here are works by Caravaggio, Van Dyck, Filippino Lippi, Murillo, Rubens and Veronese, as well as Ligurian artists Cambiaso, Magnasco and Strozzi. The 16th-century building was built for the Grimaldi family, and its white façade was added in the 18th century. There is a very pretty roof garden and café.
ⓐ Via Garibaldi 18 ☎ 010 5572013 🌐 www.museidigenova.it
🕐 09.00–19.00 Tues–Fri, 10.00–19.00 Sat & Sun, closed Mon
ⓘ Admission charge

Palazzo Ducale (Doge's Palace)

This is the former palace of the Doge, nominated leader of Genoa from the 13th to the 16th centuries. It stands in Piazza Matteotti, and only the wing to the left remains of the original building. The façade is 18th century. Inside the building is the atrium where beautiful porticoed courtyards were once used for magistrates' courts but which now houses a café. You can visit the public rooms including the Doge's chapel. There are changing exhibitions – such as 'Mediterraneo' (from Courbet to Matire) until 2011 – but it's also home to the Museo del Jazz (Jazz Museum), which tells the history of jazz and its leading musicians. ⓐ Piazza Matteotti 9 ☎ Palace: 010 5574000; Jazz Museum: 010 585241
🌐 www.palazzoducale.genova.it 🕐 Palace: 09.00–21.00 Tues–Sun, closed Mon; Jazz Museum: 16.00–19.00 Mon–Sat, closed Sun
ⓘ Admission charge for exhibitions (Palace)

◆ *One of the many exhibits at the Palazzo Ducale*

Palazzo Rosso (Red Palace)

Genoa had some generous, rich people. This collection was donated to the city by the Brignole-Sale family and is housed in a *palazzo* that is a work of art in itself with 17th-century frescoes. Fortunately for the city, the original designs of the palace were left intact when the place was bombed by the Allies in World War II. Much of what you see is a 1950s reconstruction. To do justice to the collection you need at least an afternoon. Paintings to look out for are *Portrait of a Young Man* by Dürer, several works by Van Dyck, *Judith and Holofernes* by Paolo Veronese and *The Cook* by Bernardo Strozzi. From the roof (there is a lift) there are lovely views over the city. ⓐ Via Garibaldi 18 ⓣ 010 246351 ⓦ www.museidigenova.it ⓒ 09.00–19.00 Tues–Fri, 10.00–19.00 Sat & Sun, closed Mon ⓘ Admission charge

RETAIL THERAPY

The shopping highlight for the label-conscious is Via Roma, where all the big names hang out, including Dolce & Gabbana, Mario Forn (for Prada), Ferragamo and Louis Vuitton, as well as many individual, but pricey, boutiques. All the shops along Via Roma are closed all day Sunday as well as Monday morning.

Andrea Morando Stylish leather boots, bags and accessories from the likes of Burberry, Church's and Tod's. ⓐ Via XXV Aprile 47r and 54r ⓣ 010 2543888 ⓒ 09.30–12.30, 15.00–19.30 Mon–Sat, closed Sun

...**Scurreria** Beautiful and unusual homeware at
...onable prices. ⓐ Via Scurreria 17 R ① 010 2470293
① 09.00–13.00 & 15.30–9.30 Mon–Sat, closed Sun

La Bottega Solidale Fair-trade store selling all the usual things
– coffee and chocolate, soft toys, clothes, basketware and
perfume. ⓐ Via Galata 122r, off Via XX Setembre ① 010 8685468
ⓦ www.bottegasolidale.it ① 15.30–19.30 Mon, 09.30–19.30
Tues–Fri, 09.30–12.30 Sat, 15.30–19.30 Sun

Gismondi Nice crockery shop, full of things that would make
your kitchen look continental. Also some pretty jewellery, glass
and pots. ⓐ Via Galata 102r, off Via XX Setembre ① 010 5960322
ⓦ www.gismondilamaison.it ① 09.15–12.30, 14.30–19.30 Tues–Sat,
closed Sun & Mon

Sartù The designer sits inside threading pretty pieces of things
together to make some stunning jewellery. Also bags and clothes.
ⓐ Via Luccoli 80–82r ① 010 252268 ⓦ www.sartubijoux.it
① 09.00–13.00, 14.00–19.30 Mon–Sat, closed Sun

TAKING A BREAK

Trattoria da Maria £ ❶ Generally agreed to be the most
authentic food in town, this ancient restaurant groans with
customers at lunchtime, won't take reservations and puts all its
customers together on long, bare benches. The family go to the
market early each morning to buy their ingredients, cook them
all up and post the dishes available all over the walls, taking them

down as the dishes run out. If you're upstairs your food will arrive via the dumb waiter. Lots of fun. ➌ Vico Testadore 14r, off Via XXV Aprile ❶ 010 581080 ❷ 11.45–15.00 Mon–Sat, closed Sun

Garibaldi £–££ ❷ A café bar and restaurant set in the lobby of the 17th-century Durazzo palace, with wonderful marble pillars and cosy nooks for quiet mid-morning coffee and snacks. Excellent-value buffet lunch for €8 served from 12.30–15.00. Check this place out too for the buffet *aperitivi* (from 17.00) and dinner menu. ➍ Via al Quattro Canti di San Francesco 40r ❶ 010 2470847 Ⓦ www.garibaldicafe.it ❷ 12.30–15.00, 17.00–01.00 daily ❶ Closed throughout August

AFTER DARK

RESTAURANTS
Ristorante Stallone £ ❸ Unusually for Genoa, this place stays open till 02.00 every day. Local specialities – dried codfish stew, paella and fresh fish dishes. ➍ Piazza Brignole 2–3r ❶ 010 582456 Ⓦ www.ristorantestallone.it ❷ 12.00–15.00, 19.00–02.00 daily

Il Guscio £–££ ❹ Perfect for an aperitif, for lunch or dinner, Guscio is a smart but very reasonably priced option. Pizzas are excellent. ➍ Via XII Ottobre 196 R ❶ 010 5958496 Ⓦ www.ristoranteilguscio.it ❷ 12.00–01.00 Mon–Fri, 18.00–01.00 Sat & Sun

La Cantina Squarciafico ££ ❺ Down steps into a warm, brick-walled wine cellar in an old mansion with quiet background music and a small menu of innovative Ligurian cuisine. Extensive wine list. ⓐ Piazza Invrea 3r ⓣ 010 2470823 ⓦ www.squarcifico.it ⓛ 12.30–14.00, 19.00–23.00 daily

Le Rune ££ ❻ This modern, brightly lit, Michelin-listed place offers a new take on Ligurian cuisine. A four-course menu changes daily, or you can choose from the standard menu. Lots of home-made pastas served with various sauces and plenty of fish on the menu, including an excellent mixed seafood starter. Good vegetarian options – look for ravioli stuffed with mushrooms and spinach sauce. Excellent service and no background music, but if you want a bit of space, head upwards. ⓐ Vico Domoculta 14r, near Via XXV Aprile ⓣ 010 594951 ⓛ 12.30–14.30, 19.30–22.30 daily

Chichibio £££ ❼ This place comes highly recommended for good value and thoughtful cooking. A long spacious dining room, minimalist décor, glass tables and perspex chairs make for an interesting atmosphere. ⓐ Via David Chiossone 20r ⓣ 010 2476191 ⓦ www.chichibio.ge.it ⓛ 12.30–14.00, 19.00–23.00 Mon–Sat, closed Sun

I Tre Merli £££ ❽ One of two branches of the same place (the other is down in Porto Antico, close to Il Bigo). This is an old wine cellar serving an upmarket version of traditional Ligurian cuisine. Home-made pasta, smoked meat and cheeses. Nice place for a romantic dinner. ⓐ Vico dietro il Coro della Maddalena ⓣ 010 247 4095 ⓦ www.itremerli.it ⓛ 12.30–15.00, 19.30–23.00 Mon–Fri, 19.30–23.00 Sat, closed Sun

Via Balbi & around

This area to the west of the city is less clearly defined than the other two districts. It is dominated by Via Balbi, established in the early 17th century under an agreement by the powerful Balbi family and the city government. Seven *palazzi* were built here, and most of them are still intact, though not all are open to the public. The area is home to the university and several inexpensively priced hotels, as well as Palazzo Principe and Palazzo Reale, more of the city's grand *palazzi*. Back in the harbour there's the ultra-modern Galata Museo del Mare, and further out of town is Righi and the parkland surrounding the old city fortifications. Across to the west is the symbol of the city – La Lanterna, the old lighthouse, now in the process of being converted to a museum. A trip to the west of the city brings you to Parco Durazzo Pallavicini, an 11-hectare (27-acre) park filled with statuary.

SIGHTS & ATTRACTIONS

Basilica di San Francesco di Paola

A visit to this 16th-century church is well worth the time for the views over Genoa and Porto Antico as much as for the church itself. In its time the church was an important one, patronised by many of the influential families in the city. Sailors traditionally came here to ask for protection while at sea, and it contains many *ex votos*, little tokens left by sailors, as well as some significant artworks. The road up to the church from the harbour is marked out with the Stations of the Cross. **ⓐ** Piazza San Francesco do Paola 4 **ⓘ** 010 261228 **ⓛ** 08.00–12.30, 15.00–18.00 daily **ⓝ** Bus: 32

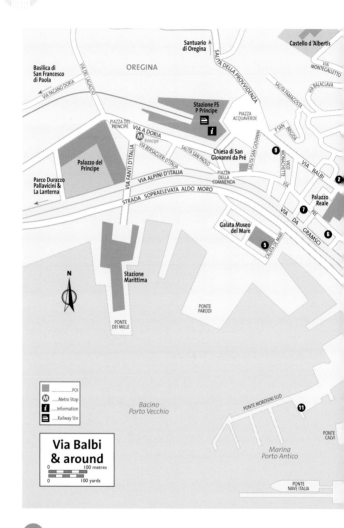

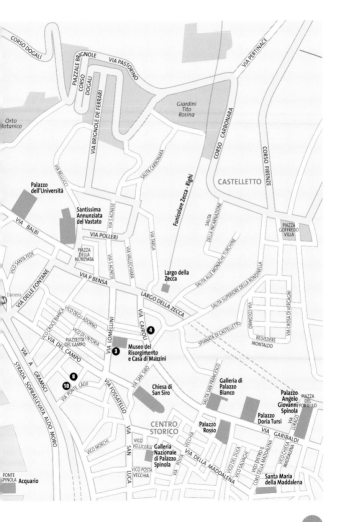

CORSO DOGALI

PIAZZALE BAIGNOLE

CORSO DOGALI

VIA PASTORINO

VIA PERTINACE

VIA BRIGNOLE DE FERRARI

Orto Botanico

Giardini Tito Rosina

CASTELLETTO

CORSO CARBONARA

CORSO FIRENZE

VIA BELLUCCI

Palazzo dell'Università

SALITA CARBONARA

SALITA DELLA INCARNAZIONE

PIAZZA GOFFREDO VILLA

VIA BALBI

Santissima Annunziata del Vastato

VIA S. AGNESE

Funicolare Zecca - Righi

VIA POLLERI

VIA TARGA

VICO SANTA FEDE

VIA DELLE FONTANE

PIAZZA DELLA NUNZIATA

VIA P. BENSA

VIA S. AGNESE

VIA VALLECHIARA

Largo della Zecca

SALITA ALLE MONACHE TURCHINE

Darsena

VICO CROCE BIANCA

VICO DEGLI ADORNO

LARGO DELLA ZECCA

SALITA SUPERIORE DELLA ROMONELLA

VICO DI LUNTORIA

VIA LOMELLINI

VIA CAIROLI

VIA COLOMBO

VIA CROSA DI VERGAGNI

VIA DEL CAMPO

PIAZZETTA DEL CAMPO

SPIANATA DI CASTELLETTO

BELVEDERE MONTALDO

VIA A. GRAMSCI

Museo del Risorgimento e Casa di Mazzini ❹

STRADA SOPRAELEVATA ALDO MORO

❸

❽

VIA SAN SIRO

❿

VIA PONTE CALVI

VIA FOSSATELLO

SALITA SAN FRANCESCO

Chiesa di San Siro

Galleria di Palazzo Bianco

Palazzo Angelo Giovanni Spinola

PIAZZA DEL PORTELLO

VICO LUCCOLI

VIA LOMELLINI

VIA SAN LUCA

VICO MORCHI

CENTRO STORICO

Palazzo Rosso

Palazzo Doria Tursi

VIA GARIBALDI

VICO PELLICCERIA

VICO POSTA VECCHIA

Galleria Nazionale di Palazzo Spinola

VIA SAN LUCA

VIA DELLA MADDALENA

VICO DELLA MADDALENA

VICO CHIESA MADDALENA

Santa Maria della Maddalena

PONTE SPINOLA

Acquario

Castello d'Albertis (Albertis Castle)

This is one of the highlights of a visit to the city, partly for the lovely interior of the building, partly for the views from its gardens and partly for the journey upwards towards it. The late 19th-century neo-Gothic fortified house was built by the man whose name it bears. He was an explorer and navigator and gave his house and collection of ethnographical pieces to the city in the 1930s. But better than the native American artefacts and the pots and armour is the house itself, its library, sitting room and dining room intact, with glorious views of the city. The gardens offer a lovely view of the port. ❸ Corso Dogali 18 ☎ 010 2723820 ⓦ www.museidigenova.it ⏱ 10.00–18.00 Tues–Fri, 10.00–19.00 Sat & Sun (Apr–Sept); 10.00–17.00 Tues–Fri, 10.00–18.00 Sat & Sun (Oct–Mar) Ⓝ Bus: 39, 40 ❶ Admission charge

Chiesa di San Giovanni da Pré (Church of San Giovanni da Pré)

This 14th-century double-decker church was built by the Knights of the Order of St John as a dual-purpose building. It consists of two churches, one built on top of the other. The upper storey was originally for the private use of the knights. Next door is a hostel built by the knights for pilgrims en route to the Holy Land. It has been restored to its 16th-century appearance. The building is used as an exhibition centre. ❸ Piazza della Commenda 1 ☎ 010 265486 ⓦ www.irolli.it ⏱ 08.00–12.30, 15.00–19.00 daily

Chiesa di San Siro (Church of San Siro)

A church has stood on this spot since the 4th century, but the current building was created in the 16th century after fire

⬤ *The neo-Gothic Castello d'Albertis*

destroyed the earlier building. Until the 9th century, when
San Lorenzo was built, the city's cathedral stood here. San Lorenzo,
deep inside the city walls, was considered a safer location. Badly
damaged in World War II, the interior has been restored in the
highly elaborate style of the 16th and 17th centuries. ⓐ Via San
Siro 3 ⓣ 010 2461674 ⓛ 08.00–12.00, 15.00–19.00 daily

City walls & fortifications

In the 17th century, at the height of its power, Genoa faced the
threat of invasion by France and the House of Savoy, and so great
walls and battlements were built in an arc in the hills surrounding
the city. Looking up on a clear day, quite a lot of this can be seen.
Some of the walls are rather inaccessible and can be visited only
by guided tour, but you can take the funicular railway to Righi,
where marked walking trails lead to forts Begato, Sperone, Puin
and Diamante. ⓝ Funicular: Largo della Zecca

⬥ *La Lanterna is a unique Genoese landmark*

Galata Museo del Mare (Galata Sea Museum)

Part of the redevelopment of the old port, this museum, built in 2004, tells the story of Genoa as a port and seafaring city, and its main exhibit is a restored 16th-century galley. A reconstruction of a 17th-century pirate ship is a great draw for children. The museum is interactive, so you can experience what being at sea must have been like. A recent addition is a real submarine docked outside the museum since 2010, which offers a full submersion experience. ⓐ Calata de Mari ⓣ 010 2345666 ⓦ www.galatamuseodelmare.it ⓛ 10.00–19.30 Tues–Sun, closed Mon (Mar–Oct); 10.00–18.00 Tues–Fri, 10.00–19.30 Sat & Sun, closed Mon (Nov–Feb) ⓘ Open till 22.00 Fridays in August. Admission charge

La Lanterna (The Lighthouse)

There has been a lighthouse here since the 12th century. The current tower, which was built in 1543, rises to 117 m (384 ft) above sea level, and you can climb the 172 steps to the first terrace. The base has been converted into a museum dedicated to the history and culture of Genoa. A promenade across the quays takes you out to the tower. ⓐ Via Milano ⓣ 010 910001 ⓦ www.liguri.org/lanterna ⓛ Promenade and park: 08.00–sunset daily; museum: 10.00–19.00 Sat & Sun, closed Mon–Fri

Palazzo dell'Università (University Palace)

A former Jesuit college built in the 17th century, this building now belongs to the university, and it is worth venturing inside to see the Great Hall, atrium and hanging gardens. ⓐ Via Balbi ⓣ 010 20991 ⓛ 07.00–19.00 Mon–Fri, 07.00–12.00 Sat, closed Sun

Parco Durazzo Pallavicini (Durazzo Pallavicini Park)

This 11-hectare (27-acre) 19th-century park includes a Chinese pagoda, lots of follies, a temple of Diana set in an artificial lake, a fantasy castle (not open to the public) and hundreds of exotic plants. Via Pallavicini 13, Pegli 010 6981048 09.00–19.00 daily (Apr–Sept); 09.00–17.00 daily (Oct–Mar) Bus: 1, 2, 3 from Stazione Principe

Santissima Annunziata del Vastato

Set outside the city walls, this church was built for the Lomellini clan during the 16th and 17th centuries. The interior of the church is richly decorated, with much of the original work remaining intact, and includes work by several important local artists of the 16th and 17th centuries. Piazza della Nunziata 4 010 2465525 www.irolli.it 07.30–12.30, 15.00–19.00 daily

Santuario di Oregina

Another spectacularly sited church. This one looks out over the whole city and port area. The building dates back to the 17th century and belonged to a Franciscan order. Originally intended as a simple Franciscan hermitage, over time a dome, Corinthian columns and some noteworthy paintings were added. At Christmas the church is visited for its Nativity scene, with models dating back to the 18th century. At the bottom of the steps leading up to the church is a pleasant little square that would make a good place for a picnic. Salita Oregina 44 010 212024 08.30–12.00, 15.00–19.00 daily Bus: 39

○ *Neptune's statue adorns the gardens of the Palazzo del Principe*

CULTURE

Palazzo del Principe (Prince's Palace)

Built by the Admiral Andrea Doria and his descendants from
the early 16th century, the Palazzo is, amazingly, still owned by
them. It was decorated by Perin del Vaga, a pupil of Raphael. The
public rooms contain some interesting portraits, including one
attributed to Titian and another portrait in which they think
Rubens painted the hands. You can visit the private rooms of
Andrea Doria and there are some mildly interesting tapestries
of the Battle of Lepanto, made in Brussels in the 16th century.
The highlight of the exhibitions is a portrait of *Doria as Neptune*
by Bronzino. Outside, the gardens with their great 16th-century
marble statue of Neptune are beautifully tended. There is a
sweeping vista from the roof terrace, which was once the
Dorias' personal quayside. ⓐ Piazza del Principe 4 ⓣ 010 255509
ⓦ www.dopart.it ⓛ 10.00–17.00 Tues–Sun, closed Mon &
public holidays

Palazzo Reale

The spectacular 18th-century Galleria degli Specchi is the hall
of mirrors where the Balbi family, after whom the street is
named, used to entertain their guests. The royal house of
Savoy got hold of it in 1825, and all their belongings and a
few additions now make up a museum of ballrooms, audience
chambers, throne room, frescoes and one or two rather nice
pieces of art, especially the Van Dycks. There are wonderful
views over the harbour and from the terrace, and a pretty
garden containing a recycled mosaic. ⓐ Via Balbi 10

ⓣ 010 27101 ⓦ www.palazzorealegenova.it ⓛ 09.00–13.30
Tues & Wed, 09.00–19.00 Thur–Sun, closed Mon
ⓘ Admission charge

RETAIL THERAPY

This area is a bit short on opportunities for suitcase fillers
but there are some interesting moments along Via da Pré
and Via del Campo, mostly ethnic supermarkets run by
the city's recently arrived African population, and some
temporary-looking, very inexpensive clothes shops with
lots of cheap T-shirts.

Foccaceria di Via Lomellini Excellent bakery in this street full of
places to check out. Get there in the morning when the counters
are heaving with focaccia, pizzas and cakes. ⓐ Via Lomellini 57r
ⓣ 010 2461448 ⓛ 07.30–19.30 Mon–Sat, closed Sun

Gurrieri An old-fashioned shoe shop where you can
get lovely handmade sensible shoes at reasonable prices.
ⓐ Via Lomellini 5r ⓣ 010 2511889 ⓛ 09.30–12.30, 15.30–19.30
Mon–Sat, closed Sun

Pandemonio Two shops close by one another with lots of
interesting women's fashions at just about affordable prices.
ⓐ Via Lomellini 22r/Piazza della Nunziata 6r ⓣ 010 2465901/010
2465494 ⓦ www.pandemonio.biz ⓛ 09.30–12.30, 15.30–19.30
Mon–Sat, closed Sun

TAKING A BREAK

Around Piazza Acquaverde and the western end of Via Balbi (the area where visitors coming by train and plane will arrive) are lots of inexpensive hotels and some good café bars. Most cafés keep very regular hours, 06.00–21.30, and close on Sundays. At 147 Via Balbi is the **HB Café** (£ ❶) which is both a shop and a café with lots of room inside, selling fresh bread, focaccia, cheeses and some groceries. At 182R is **Gianni Bar** (£ ❷), another functional place but useful for starving new arrivals, with a full restaurant menu posted up on a blackboard outside. Also handy are:

Caffè Laiolo £ ❸ Tiny, smart café bar, still in its 1938 style, selling all the usual range of bar snacks during the day and with a good reputation for *aperitivi* from 18.00–21.00. It gets extra points too for opening on the dreaded Genoa Sunday, when the place becomes a ghost town. ⓐ Via Lomellini 37r ⓣ 010 2465776 ⓛ 08.00–21.00 Tues–Sun, closed Mon

Caffè Monticelli £ ❹ One of a chain of café bars with very inexpensive snacks, good for a fast lunch of pizza or focaccia for less than €3, followed by tiramisu or strawberries and ice cream for less than €1, or just a good coffee stop. ⓐ Via Cairoli 35r ⓣ 010 2461673 ⓛ 06.00–21.00 Mon–Sat, closed Sun

Galata Café £ ❺ Set in a modern glass box above the Galata Museum, the café is a serious contender for the best *aperitivi* in town. A big balcony overlooks the harbour (and the motorway).

€10 buys a cocktail and access to the huge buffet table laid out from 18.00–22.00. Good place for a quiet coffee and snack during the day. Check out the lunch menu. ⓐ Galata Museo del Mare, Primo Piano (1st floor) ⓣ 010 2543939 ⓦ www.galatacafe.com ⓛ 11.00–late daily

AFTER DARK

RESTAURANTS
Della Darsena £ ❻ Simple, inexpensive, local restaurant. Try seafood risotto or penne with pesto. Not a place for a candlelit dinner, but it has a playroom for children. ⓐ Via Pré 86r ⓣ 010 256625 ⓛ 12.00–15.00, 18.00–21.00 Tues–Sun, closed Mon

Mamacita's Taqueria £ ❼ Excellent Mexican restaurant located off Via Balbi on Via Pré. Expect tacos, nachos, quesadillas and, of course, tequila. ⓐ Via Pré 11 R ⓛ 11.30–15.30 & 18.30–21.00 Mon–Fri & 12.00–21.00 Sat, closed Sun

Al Veliero ££ ❽ Quiet place with a good standing, serving mainly fish but with ample offerings for carnivores. Similar in style to Le Maschere just down the road, so check out both of them for the specials. Cover charge of €2.50. ⓐ Via Ponte Calvi 10r ⓣ 010 2465773 ⓛ 12.30–18.00, 19.30–24.00 Tues–Sun, closed Mon

Lupo Antica Trattoria £££ ❾ This place is one of the more innovative places to eat in the city. Seafood-dominated, but there are beef and veal options and vegetarians can rummage out a tasty meal too. The menu includes an English translation so

you'll have no unpleasant surprises. ⓐ Vico Monachette 20r
ⓣ 010 267036 ⓦ www.lupoanticatrattoria.it ⓛ 12.30–18.00,
19.30–24.00 Mon–Sat, closed Sun

Le Maschere £££ ⑩ Very typical Ligurian cuisine, doing some
excellent lunch offers but also good for an evening meal. Pretty,
quiet interior, white cloths, uniformed staff, menu posted up in
English. Like most Genoese restaurants, the menu is mostly fish
but there are also lots of meaty standards. ⓐ Via Al Ponte Calvi
2–4r ⓣ 010 2465503 ⓛ 12.30–18.00, 19.30–24.00 Mon–Sat,
closed Sun

Da Toto £££ ⑪ Very classy restaurant at the end of Ponte
Morosini with some grand views of the millions of euros worth
of yachts anchored all around. A new take on the classic cuisine
of Genoa with lots of seafood options cooked in creative sauces,
as well as steak and veal and even several vegetarian options.
Reservations recommended. ⓐ Ponte Morosini Sud
ⓣ 010 2543870 ⓦ www.ristorantedatoto.it ⓛ 12.00–15.00,
20.00–23.00 daily

BARS
La Cattiva Strada Deep in the dark heart of the Old City, this tiny
bar has seats out on the *piazzetta*, live music ranging from
South American guitar to Bossa Nova on Fridays and Saturdays
and *aperitivi* worth seeking out. ⓐ Piazzetta del Campo 1r
ⓣ 010 2474304 ⓛ 07.00–21.00 daily

◗ *Portofino's colourful harbour*

OUT OF TOWN
trips

Portofino & Santa Margherita Ligure

Two seaside resorts, the former a tiny fishing village that has attracted the glitterati and the latter a classic tourist-oriented town with pebbly beach, bathing huts and affordable restaurants. Both have gorgeous blue sea, palm trees, rocky inlets and both charge for the use of the beach. For more information see ⓦ www.comune.portofino.genova.it

GETTING THERE

Access to Santa Margherita Ligure is from Stazione Principe or Brignole eastwards on trains to La Spezia. Access to Portofino is either by tour boat or by train to Santa Margherita Ligure and then a bus ride round the single-track coastal road. Car drivers will find themselves queuing for hours to get a parking space. In summer a more scenic, if slower and more expensive, way of arriving at Portofino or Santa Margherita is by ferry. **Consorzio Liguria Via Mare** boats (❶ 010 256775 ⓦ www.liguriaviamare.it) leave from beside the Aquarium May–Sept. The **tourist office** in Santa Margherita Ligure is at ❸ Via XXV Aprile 2B ❶ 0185 287485 ⓦ www.apttigullio.liguria.it ❹ 09.30–12.30, 15.00–19.30 daily (May–Sept); 09.30–12.30, 15.00–17.30 daily (Oct–Apr)

SIGHTS & ATTRACTIONS

Chiesa di San Giorgio (Church of St George), Portofino
This is a 19th-century church up behind the main village with some beautiful mosaic-pebbled areas in front of it. Local people

believe that those who marry here will never be happily married, but that might have a lot to do with the fact that lots of celebrity weddings take place here. Inside are relics of St George brought back from the Crusades. ⓐ Salita San Giorgio ⓛ 08.00–12.30, 15.00–19.00 daily

Parco di Portofino (Park of Portofino)

The hills surrounding Portofino are part of a national park which has a number of clearly marked trails for walks lasting between two and nine hours. They take in olive groves, tiny vineyards and gardens, chestnut woods and great vistas. ⓐ Viale

🔺 The cheerful exterior of the Chiesa di San Giorgio

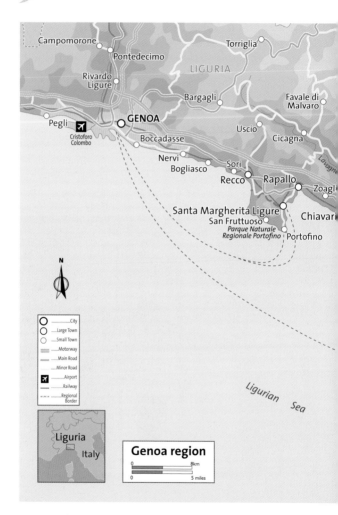

Campomorone
Pontedecimo
Torriglia
LIGURIA
Rivardo
Ligure
Bargagli
Favale di
Malvaro
Pegli
Cristoforo
Colombo
GENOA
Boccadasse
Uscio
Cicagna
Nervi
Bogliasco
Sori
Recco
Rapallo
Zoagl
Santa Margherita Ligure
Chiavar
San Fruttuoso
Parque Naturale
Regionale Portofino
Portofino

N

O ....City
O ....Large Town
O ....Small Town
........Motorway
........Main Road
........Minor Road
✈ ....Airport
........Railway
........Regional
Border

Ligurian Sea

Liguria
Italy

Genoa region
0 ....8km
0 ....5 miles

Rainusso 1, Santa Margherita Ligure ❶ 0185 289479
ⓦ www.parcoportofino.it ❶ Some of the walks are physically
demanding

Piazza del Castello (Castle Square), Santa Margherita Ligure

This attractive square is home to the Castello Sul Mare and
Chiesa dei Cappuccini, and provides some excellent views. Built
in 1150 to protect the town against pirates, the Castello is
currently used as an exhibition space, and the lower section is a
public toilet. Beside the Castello is a pretty courtyard laid out
with black and white marble pebbles in a style known as *risseu*,
which is a common decorative style around the region. From the
courtyard there are fine views over the town and the Gulf of
Tigulio. The church is 17th century. Inside is a 15th-century
crucifix. ❷ Salita al Castello ❶ 0185 283023 ❻ Castello:
10.00–13.00, 15.00–19.00 Sat & Sun; church: 07.30–12.30,
15.00–19.00 daily ❶ Admission charge

Portofino village

This is very pretty as seaside villages go. The estate in the hills to
the south of the harbour is owned by Domenico Dolce & Stefano
Gabbana, who make regular appearances. There's an excellent
walk out to the 16th-century Fortezza di San Giorgio and its
gardens and then on to the lighthouse for some fine views.
Tourist office ❷ Via Roma 35 ❶ 0185 269024

Santa Margherita Ligure town

The perfect place for a seaside holiday – plenty of great places
to eat, shops to lure you in and a lovely pebbly beach. It even

has a nightclub. It's great as a base for visits along the coast or just come out for a day trip. **Tourist office** ⓐ Via XXV Aprile 26 ⓣ 0185 287485

Villa Durazzo, Santa Margherita Ligure

The villa, set in an Italian-style garden that sits on the hill in the middle of the town, was built in the 17th century by the town's *doge*, Gio Luca Chiavari, who wanted a *palazzo* to match those in Via Garibaldi. It is now a museum, its rooms decorated as the original *doge* had them. Sights in here include the green room, the private chapel and the family apartments. Outside the house is the Chiesa di San Giacomo di Corte, an elaborate Baroque church. ⓐ Via Principe Centurione ⓣ 0185 205449 ⓦ www.durazza.it ⓛ 09.00–13.00 & 14.30–18.30 daily (summer), 14.30–17.00 daily (winter) ⓘ Admission charge

▲ *The picturesque seaside town of Santa Margherita Ligure*

THE MADONNA OF LETTERS

Inside the Chiesa di San Giacomo in Santa Margherita Ligure is a carved wooden statue of the Madonna, which legend says arrived here on its own by sea. According to the story, in 1783, an earthquake devastated Messina, and the statue in a church close to the port floated off and was carried by currents to the Gulf of Tigulio, where it washed up in Santa Margherita Ligure. This was duly taken as a sign that this was to be its new home.

RETAIL THERAPY

D&G For high-end purchases from the duo who might be popping in from their nearby holiday home. ⓐ Calata Marconi 4, Portofino ⓣ 0185 267028 ⓛ 10.00–19.00 Mon–Sat, closed Sun

Kiwi Swimwear For the beautiful people. Everything you may ever need while lying on the beach. ⓐ Via Bottaro 49, Santa Margherita Ligure ⓣ 0185 289958 ⓛ 10.00–19.00 Mon–Sat, closed Sun

Mara Sanguinetti Typical tourist shop selling Portofino souvenirs, many of which are quite attractive, including some original framed oil paintings. It's also the cheapest shop in town. ⓐ Via Roma 25, Portofino ⓣ 0185 269633 ⓛ 10.00–20.00 daily

Mingo Started off as a shoe repairers and then when the celebs arrived, they bought Mingo's line in soft-soled espadrilles and the shop has never looked back. Quaint old-fashioned shoe-shop interior; affordable shoes. ⓐ Via Roma 9, Portofino ⓣ 0185 269570 ⓛ 10.00–24.00 daily (summer); 10.00–21.00 daily (winter)

Santa Margherita Ligure market Saturday mornings see the pedestrianised streets around the city centre turn into a market for antiques and curios, old prints, junk, jewellery, original watercolours and pottery. ⓐ Via Partigiani ⓛ 10.00–14.00 Sat

Seghezzo Fratelli Vast delicatessen and supermarket selling wine, fresh vegetables, lovely cooked meats and cheeses, vegetables floating in olive oil, dried fruit, as well as toiletries and other goodies. Also the biggest cans of tuna you ever saw. This is the place to buy your picnic for Portofino. ⓐ Via Cavour 1, Santa Margherita Ligure ⓣ 0185 287172 ⓦ www.seghezzo.it ⓛ 08.00–13.00, 16.00–20.00 daily

Studio d'Arte Mara Pisano Lovely blue and green pottery relief scenes of the area, as well as more conventional pots and plates. The shop is a little way to the east of town along the coast road. ⓐ Via Dagana, Santa Margherita Ligure ⓣ 0185 283428 ⓛ 10.00–18.00 Mon–Sat, closed Sun

TAKING A BREAK

Bar San Giorgio £ Hugely popular *gelateria* in Portofino selling every imaginable ice cream. Try the house speciality, *pacingo* – strawberries, cream and strawberry ice cream. ⓐ Via Roma, Portofino ⓛ 10.00–20.00 daily

Zinco £ Modern café bar in the middle of Santa Margherita, which also does pizzas. Good for a coffee or mid-morning snack. ⓐ Via Pescino 6, Santa Margherita Ligure ⓣ 0185 280431 ⓛ 08.00–21.00 daily

Cinzia e Mario ££ Enormous restaurant in the main square of Santa Margherita, serving traditional Ligurian dishes. Lots of seafood, good vegetarian choices, pizzas and a big wine list. This place has the added advantage of a children's room as well as 27 different types of dessert. Funny fish-shaped plates. ⓐ Via Palaestro 26, Santa Margherita Ligure ⓣ 0185 287505 ⓦ www.ristorantecinziamario.it ⓛ 12.00–22.00 daily

Trattoria Tripoli ££ If you must eat or drink in Portofino, where the prices seem to include the cost of celeb-watching, this place is one of the least expensive. A cool, dark interior offers some privacy from the hordes who descend from the tour boats on an hourly basis. Mostly seafood. ⓐ Piazza Martiri dell'Olivetta 49, Portofino ⓣ 0185 269011 ⓛ 12.00–16.00, 19.30–22.30 Thur–Tues, closed Wed

AFTER DARK

RESTAURANTS
Ristorante da Michele ££ If it's just a meal you're after, the seafront at Santa Margherita Ligure is full of places. This one stands out among the crowd, with a bit more space, a readable menu and good service. ⓐ Largo Amendola 17, Santa Margherita Ligure ⓣ 0185 283660 ⓛ 12.00–14.00, 19.00–22.00 daily

Da U Batti £££ Expensive but worth it. Set in a pedestrianised, tree-lined backstreet of Portofino, most people never find their way here. Many of the tables are out in the lane. The tiny daily menu offers few choices but the food has an excellent reputation. Mostly seafood, the set dinner will set you back €75 without wine. ❸ Vico Nuovo 17, Portofino ❶ 0185 269379 ❶ 18.00–23.00 Tues–Sun, closed Mon (Mar–Nov)

Oca Bianca £££ If you've eaten all the seafood you can handle for one trip, try this place, which is seafood-free. Lots of innovative dishes using Ligurian-style cooking but with some unusual combinations. Vegetarians will do well here, and children are catered for. ❸ Via XXV Aprile 21, Santa Margherita Ligure ❶ 0185 286059 ❶ 12.00–14.00, 19.00–22.00 Tues–Sun, closed Mon

● *Enjoy Portofino's glorious setting as you sip your cappuccino*

Strainer £££ Right at the end of the pier at Portofino, this is aspiring celebrity territory. Prices are high but the food is as good as it gets around here. Traditional food such as ravioli stuffed with cheese and spinach and served with walnut sauce. Live music at weekends. Sauces are mixed up in great hollowed-out parmesan blocks to give them extra flavour. ⓐ Molo Umberto 19, Portofino ⓣ 0185 269189 ⓛ 12.00–14.30, 19.00–24.00 daily

BARS & CLUBS

Il Covo The most famous nightclub on the Ligurian coast, Il Covo is where the cool people hang out. Situated in an historic building, the luxurious club boasts a bathhouse, restaurant and club, and a guest list that includes Domenico Dolce and Stefano Gabbana. ⓐ Lungomare Rossetti ⓣ 0185 290348 ⓦ www.covodinordest.it ⓛ 20.00–04.00 daily

ACCOMMODATION

Hotel Europa £ Family-run, small place with good service and spacious, simple rooms. All rooms en-suite. ⓐ Via Trento 5, Santa Margherita Ligure ⓣ 0185 287187 ⓦ www.hoteleuropa-sml.it

Hotel Jolanda ££ Small family-run hotel with swish, overdraped rooms and a comfortable lounge. Great breakfast and a good reputation for evening meals if you want to eat in. ⓐ Lusito Costa 6, Santa Margherita Ligure ⓣ 0185 2857512 ⓦ www.hoteljolanda.it

The Cinque Terre

The five villages of the Cinque Terre are now linked to the city by roads, but for centuries the only route between them was the series of donkey trails along the coast, now very popular walking trails. Despite the crowds who turn up daily, the villages are great places to spend some time and even attempt some of the more challenging walks in the national park.

GETTING THERE

Access to the villages is by train from Genoa on the La Spezia line. If you are spending only a day here, take a fast train to Riomaggiore, the furthermost village, and return at your leisure on the slower local trains. A day ticket will allow you unlimited access to each of the stations for the day. An alternative route into the villages is by tour boat, which operates in the summer months only and is much slower but more picturesque. Boats leave from beside the Aquarium May–Sept (see page 74). A **ferry service (Consorzio Marittimo Turistico** ❶ 0187 818440 ⓦ www.navigazionegolfodeipoeti.it) also operates between the villages, but check that your ferry stops at the village you want. The ferry does not stop at Corniglia.

SIGHTS & ATTRACTIONS

Monterosso al Mare
This is the most popular and well organised of the five villages, with its rocky beach roped off into private areas and one tiny

⬥ *The hillside village of Monterosso al Mare*

patch of free beach. The village is divided into two halves by the mountain. To reach it, turn left out of the station and go through the tunnel. If, instead of passing through the tunnel, you take the pathway over the hillside, wonderful views of the coastline open up. The path goes on to the statue of St Francis and a Capuchin monastery, which has a painting of the crucifixion said to be by Van Dyck. A further walk brings you to the cemetery and the ruins of medieval fortifications. At the other end of the village, at Fegina, an enormous concrete statue of Neptune sits on the cliffs. From here to Vernazza the walking/hiking route is about an hour and a half, but it should be noted that this is hard going and not recommended for those who are not seasoned walkers.

Vernazza

This village has origins as an important harbour during the Middle Ages. Nowadays it serves as a playground for tourists, its pretty harbour filled with canoes, and its rocky beach plastered with sunbathers. History buffs can check out the church of St Margaret of Antioch, parts of which are 14th century, and the 17th-century Franciscan monastery. The challenging footpath from here to Corniglia takes about an hour and a half.

Corniglia

Even more precariously perched on the rocky hillsides above the inlet, Corniglia is cute as a button. Here you can visit the 1334 Chiesa di San Pietro (Church of St Peter), L'Oratorio dei Disciplinati di Santa Caterina (the Oratory of the Flagellants of St Catherine), which has a pretty terrace with fine views over the coast, and the remains of a castle erected in 1556. The next leg of the journey to Manarola is an easy 40 minutes.

Manarola

The village was established in the 12th century. Here among the seaside cafés and bars you can visit the 1338 Chiesa di San Lorenzo (Church of St Lawrence) and its oratory (more flagellants), built in the 14th century. The hillsides around the village are filled with vineyards and you can taste locally made wines. The footpath to Riomaggiore, known as the Via dell'Amore, takes only 20 minutes and clings to the cliff edge with stunning views all around.

Riomaggiore

Clinging to the Riomaggiore valley, the houses here seem to sit one upon the other and two tunnels link the various fragments of village together. La Chiesa di San Giovanni Battista (Church of St John the Baptist) is 14th century, and there are the remains of a castle dating back to 1260.

RETAIL THERAPY

There's not a lot in the way of purchasing opportunities in these tiny villages. A few craft shops and places selling Ligurian products will have to keep you going. Monterosso has a few dress shops and one or two other offerings.

⬤ *The wonderfully quaint harbour at Riomaggiore*

Fabbrica d'Arte Monterosso Two branches of the same shop in Monterosso al Mare. Lots of pretty ethnic pots, but the best buy is the series of relief wall plaques depicting the tortuous stacked-up village buildings. 🇦 Via V Emmanuele 27 and Via Roma 9, Monterosso al Mare 🇹 0187 817488 🇱 10.00–19.30 daily, later on Sat

La Gazza Ladra Coming upon this place on a dark evening is a little like waking up on Christmas morning when you were a child. Brightly lit, lots of jewellery, cashmere, lampshades and items to take home for friends and family. 🇦 Piazza Matteotti 6, Monterosso al Mare 🇹 0187 817068 🇱 10.00–13.00, 16.00–22.00 daily

Studio Arte Decorazione Tiny shop in Riomaggiore selling handmade rag dolls and dolls' furniture. 🇦 Via C Colombo 133 🇹 0187 760062 🇱 09.30–12.30, 14.30–19.00 daily

TAKING A BREAK

Bar Davi £ This place in Monterosso comes highly recommended if you need to find a proper fry-up breakfast (or indeed any breakfast), since they welcome tourists and cater to all their breakfast needs. It's a small bar with most of its tables out on a pleasant veranda. They also do the usual range of local food lunches, and in the evening from 16.00–22.00 you can fill up on *aperitivi*. 🇦 Via Roma 34, Monterosso 🇹 0187 817019 🇱 07.30–24.00 daily

Bar Stalin £ *Gelateria* and cake shop in Vernazza with a few tables outside and excellent ice cream. 🇦 Via Visconti 24, Vernazza 🇹 0187 812534 🇱 08.00–24.00 daily (till 19.00 winter)

🔺 *Pots and paintings at Fabbrica d'Arte Monterosso*

Trattoria Gianni Franzi ££ Sit in front of the tiny picturesque harbour in Vernazza and watch the antics of the canoeists while enjoying a drink or a coffee. Nice lunch menu in English includes lots of fish, home-made pasta, a big dessert menu and steaks. If you're interested in staying here you could ask about their accommodation. ⓐ Piazza Marconi 1, Vernazza ⓣ 0187 821003 ⓦ www.giannifranzi.it ⓛ 08.00–24.00 daily (Mar–Jan)

La Grotta ££–£££ Good place for lunch in Riomaggiore. Very traditional Ligurian food with a menu in English. Tables outside on a vine-covered veranda or inside the restaurant itself. Try the '5terre menu' – seven courses of traditional dishes, mostly fish-based, but with vegetarian choices. In the evening this place turns into a bar as well as a restaurant. ⓐ Via Colombo 123, Riomaggiore ⓣ 0187 920187 ⓛ 12.30–14.00, 18.30–22.00 daily

AFTER DARK

Baia Saracena £ Right on the port, this colourful bar/café is a useful stop for coffee or a plate of pasta. ⓐ Piazza Guglielmo Marconi 16, Vernazze ● 10.00–23.00 daily

Enoteca da Eliseo £ Outside tables set up on a square. Great for drinks and nibbles. ⓐ Piazza Maltetti 3, Monterosso ● 0187 817308 ● 12.00–22.00 daily

Osteria del Pirata ££ Long, low wine cellar serving fairly standard Ligurian dishes. Quiet compared to Ciak around the corner, but it has a gentle mood of its own, a menu in English and meat as well as seafood options. You could also try this place for lunch – the pizzas are good. ⓐ Via Vittorio Emanuele 5, Monterosso al Mare ● 12.00–14.00, 19.00–21.50 daily

Ciak £££ Full every night, this place offers a huge menu of seafood in an oriental style. If you go round to the road and peek in the kitchen window, you can watch the chef with seafood piled up all around him hurling the stuff into woks. ⓐ Piazza don Minzoni, Monterosso al Mare ● 0187 817014 ● 12.00–15.00, 19.00–24.00 daily

ACCOMMODATION

Aquamarina £ A central agency in Monterosso, which has rooms to rent for two or more days. Many are small apartments with cooking facilities, excellent for families or several people sharing. Check the website, since the standard of accommodation varies.

🅐 Via Mollinelli 27, Monterosso al Mare 🕾 338 7073664
🅦 www.corrado5terre.com

Gianni Franzi Rooms £–££ From €45 for a single room with bath and balcony and sea view. 🅐 Piazza G Marconi 5, Vernazza
🕾 0187 812228 🅦 www.giannifranzi.it

Cà dei Duxi ££ Small hotel in the main street in Riomaggiore. Six simple, clean rooms, with a website so you can book in advance. 🅐 Via Colombo 36 🕾 0187 920036 🅦 www.duxi.it

Il Maestrale ££ Set in a 16th-century *palazzo* in Monterosso, this is a comfortable family-run place with only five bedrooms. It has its own restaurant and is away from the village. 🅐 Via Roma 37
🕾 0187 817013 🅦 www.locandamaestrale.net

▶ *Fishing boats in Cinque Terre*

PRACTICAL
information

Directory

GETTING THERE

By air

Cristoforo Colombo Airport (ⓐ Genova Sestri Ponente ☏ 010 60151 ⓦ www.airport.genova.it) is linked to most major European cities as well as to Britain via British Airways and Ryanair.

BA ⓦ www.britishairways.com

Ryanair ⓦ www.ryanair.com

Many people are aware that air travel emits CO_2, which contributes to climate change. You may be interested in the possibility of lessening the environmental impact of your flight through the charity **Climate Care** (ⓦ www.jpmorganclimatecare.com), which offsets your CO_2 by funding environmental projects around the world.

By rail

From Britain, Eurostar travels from London to Paris and from there via Nice to Genoa.

Eurostar ☏ 0875 186186 ⓦ www.eurostar.com

Rail Europe ⓦ www.raileurope.co.uk (UK)

ⓦ www.eurorailways.com (US)

Thomas Cook European Rail Timetable

☏ 01733 416477 (UK) ⓦ www.thomascookpublishing.com

By road

Genoa is linked by motorway to the other major cities of Europe and by ferry or Eurotunnel to Britain. The main driving route from Genoa to the UK is via Milan and the Mont Blanc tunnel.

By water

Ferries arrive into Genoa from destinations in Italy, Corsica, Elba, Tunis and Barcelona. Ferries tend to operate during the summer months only. They arrive at the **Stazione Marittima Porto di Genova** (ⓘ 010 2412534 Ⓦ www.porto.genova.it)

Ferry companies include:

Grimaldi ⓘ 010 2094591 Ⓦ www.gnv.it

Tirrenia ⓘ 199 123199 Ⓦ www.tirrenia.it

ENTRY FORMALITIES

EU, US, Australian and New Zealand citizens do not need visas for stays of up to three months. Visitors must register with the police within three days of arriving in the city. This formality is carried out when you check in at your hotel. If you are staying with friends you must go into the local police station and register in person.

EU citizens do not have to declare goods imported or exported as long as they are for their personal use and they have arrived from within the EU. For non-EU citizens the following restrictions apply: 400 cigarettes or 200 small cigars or 500 grams of tobacco; 1 litre of spirits or 2 litres of fortified wine; 20 grams of perfume; €10,000 cash.

MONEY

Italy is a member of the European Union with the euro as its currency. This has seven banknotes: €5, €10, €20, €50, €100, €200 and €500. Coins come in denominations of €1, €2 and 1, 2, 5, 10, 20 and 50 cents. Most banks have 24-hour cashpoints (called *bancomats*) located outside and these will accept cards with

Cirrus and Maestro symbols. You can also use the ATMs to withdraw cash using Visa, Access and MasterCard. Bank opening hours are 08.20–13.20, 14.30–16.00 Monday to Friday. Banks close on public holidays and often work shorter hours on the day preceding a bank holiday.

Sterling and dollar users might want to consider traveller's cheques, which can be exchanged in banks or bureaux de change, or at some hotels if you are a guest, but these places charge a commission.

Bureaux de change open later than banks, but will probably charge for each exchange you make rather than take a percentage of the value. Their rate may not be as beneficial to you as a bank.

Post Offices (*ufficio postale*) charge €2.50 for all exchanges, regardless of the amount.

HEALTH, SAFETY & CRIME

No special precautions are required before visiting Italy. Water is safe to drink, although everyone buys bottled water. If you see the sign *acqua non potabile* on taps in toilets or on trains it means that the water is not safe to drink. The most common cause of illness (besides a hangover) is dehydration and sunburn. You should use sunscreen, wear a hat and sunglasses in summer and carry enough water at all times. Take any medication you need with you. EU citizens are entitled to the same healthcare as Italians, although you must bring a European Health Insurance Card (EHIC) and a form of identification with you. The website for ordering these cards is ⓦ www.ehic.org.uk. This card replaces the old E111 form. Private medical insurance is vital, both for non-EU citizens and also for citizens of EU states, since medicine and

▲ *Boats moored in Genoa harbour*

HEALTH INFORMATION

Ⓦ www.fco.gov.uk/travel is an informative website that provides health and general travel advice for British citizens.

Ⓦ www.cdc.gov/travel and Ⓦ www.healthfinder.com are websites geared towards American travellers.

Ⓦ www.travelhealth.co.uk has useful tips and information for British travellers.

Ⓦ www.farmacie.it is a list of pharmacies in Italy with their opening hours.

medical tests will not be covered, nor will the cost of repatriation in case of emergency. Everyone is entitled to free emergency medical care. Your hotel reception will be able to assist if you need to consult a GP who speaks English. Pharmacies, recognisable by the green cross outside, and the word *Farmacia*, open 08.30–13.00, 16.00–20.00 Monday to Saturday, and can advise on non-prescription medication. In Genoa, a rota pinned up at the entrance will indicate which pharmacy is open out of hours. Dental emergency treatment is available at Accident & Emergency, but any other dental treatment is not covered by the EHIC.

Street crime happens in every big city and it would be foolish not to take a few simple precautions. If you have a car, make sure it is parked in a secure location with lots of passers-by, and put valuables out of sight. Be particularly careful when using cashpoint machines. The area around the two rail stations can be a little dodgy at night when the people congregate, and the streets around Via della Maddalena have become a red-light and drug-dealing area. Don't assume because the streets are pedestrianised that traffic won't come along, and be prepared for motorcycle-driving handbag snatchers. Make photocopies of the important pages of your passport, travel insurance documents and traveller's cheque numbers and keep them separate from your other valuables.

There are two kinds of police in Genoa: *carabinieri* and *polizia*. *Carabinieri* (blue shirts and black trousers with a red stripe) are responsible for order on the streets, while the *polizia* (white belts) deal with bigger crimes. A subsection of the *carabinieri* is the *vigili urbani*, the traffic police (blue uniforms, white helmets). Any of them will help if you are in difficulty. If you are robbed and want to make an insurance claim, you must get a statement from the police.

OPENING HOURS

See pages 126 and 128 for banking hours and pharmacies. Smaller post offices generally open 08.00–14.00 Monday to Friday, 09.30–13.00 Saturday. Larger branches are open 08.00–19.00 Monday to Friday, 09.30–13.00 Saturday.

With some variations, museums open 09.00–17.00, while some of the very busy ones open until 23.00 in summer.

Shops in Genoa more or less open from 09.30–12.30, and then from 15.30 or 16.00 (in summer) until 19.30. Along Via XX Settembre, larger shops do not close for lunch. In Via Roma shops open at 14.00 on Mondays. Grocery stores open earlier and close earlier. Markets open considerably earlier and close around midday. In the towns and villages along the coast, shops open until late in the evening, but many of them observe the long lunch hour.

TOILETS

There are public toilets at the airport, the two railway stations and at most of the sights, although it's hard work finding some of them. If you are in the street and need to spend a penny, your best bet is to visit a café or one of the larger bars.

CHILDREN

Children are welcome everywhere in Genoa. Even the classiest restaurants provide high chairs, and lots of places have special child-friendly areas or even playrooms where they can play while you eat. Disposable nappies, baby milk and sterilising solution are all readily available in supermarkets. You should bring any medication with you such as child painkillers, inhalers or antihistamine.

Genoa is a great place for children to enjoy. The *caruggi* are good fun to explore with their unusual shops selling things to eat, and *gelaterie* can be found at regular intervals. There are lots of sights that children will enjoy – the double-decker train ride out to the eastern coast is another experience, and clambering over rocks will engage them for hours. Funicular railways are good fun, in winter there is ice-skating at Porto Antico, and the electric train that shuttles tourists around the sights is slow but engaging. And, on the subject of slow but engaging, Bigo (see page 58) may not be exactly a scary, white-knuckle ride, but children will enjoy peering down into the works as the lift grinds its way up to its impressive ultimate altitude. Who needs the delights offered by a cartoon mouse whose voice still hasn't broken when you can enjoy the fish, birds and dolphins of Genoa's Aquarium (see page 74)?

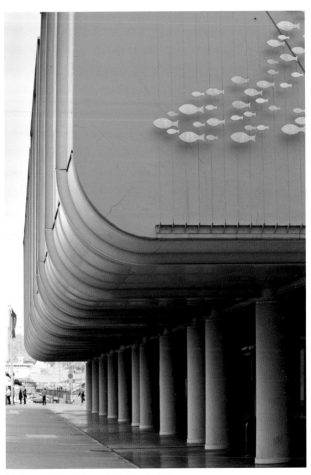

⬤ The Aquarium is the perfect place for kids

In conveniently close proximity to the Aquarium is La Sfera (see page 81). Just the shape of this curious place will whet juvenile appetites, and, once inside, their attention will be held by butterflies and jungle plants, too. The more whimsical infant will be delighted to learn that this magnificent structure was designed by a certain Mr Piano!

If you have children whose ages cover a relatively wide spectrum, it can sometimes be tricky to find a venue that has attractions to keep them all entertained; but such a place is **La Città dei Bambini** (🅐 Magazzini de Cotone, Porto Antico 🅣 010 2345635 🅦 www.cittadeibambini.net). Here, three separate zones, aimed at ages 3 to 14, mix education with play. There are knobs to press, ant farms to observe, and organised (and very informative) demonstrations.

COMMUNICATIONS
Internet
Since everyone has their own computer these days, the Internet cafés are fast disappearing in Genoa, and have given way to shops that sell cheap phone calls and have Internet stations as well. Most of these are scattered around the streets connecting to Via della Maddalena. Along the coast there are Internet cafés in most villages.

Phone
Public phone boxes take cash or *schede telefoniche* (phonecards), which can be bought at newsstands or *tabacchi* (tobacconists). Phone calls are cheaper after 18.30 and cheaper still after 22.00. You can also buy phonecards displaying an 0800 number, which

TELEPHONING GENOA
The international country code for Italy is 39, preceded by
the international code (oo from UK and New Zealand, o11
from the USA, oo11 from Australia). The city code for Genoa
is o10.

TELEPHONING ABROAD
Dial oo, the international access code followed by your
country code and then the area code minus the initial
zero followed by the number itself. Country codes:

UK: 44	Ireland: 353	France: 33
Germany: 49	USA: 1	Canada: 1
Australia: 61	New Zealand: 64	South Africa: 27

allows you to make inexpensive international calls. Phone calls
made from hotel rooms are expensive.

Post

When sending letters most people use *Posta Prioritaria*, which is
a little more expensive, needs a special sticker and has to be put
into a separate box, which is either marked *Posta Prioritaria* or
coloured blue. Postboxes are red and have two slots – one for
destinations within the city (*per la città*) and one for all other
destinations. Stamps can be bought in the *tabacchi*.

ELECTRICITY

Electrical current in Italy is 220V AC and plugs are two-pin and
round-pronged. Bringing an adaptor with you is vital since

shops in Genoa sell adaptors for Italian–British connections and not the other way round.

TRAVELLERS WITH DISABILITIES

As a city, Genoa is not particularly wheelchair-friendly, since many of the *caruggi* have steps. However, all new buildings in the city are, by law, wheelchair-friendly. For detailed information on what is accessible contact **Terre di Mare** (ⓦ www.terredimare.it), which is a regularly updated website in Italian and English aimed at tourists with disabilities. They also have an information point in the city at Palazzo Ducale. The airport has disabled access toilets, as do the two railway stations. The **Italian Ministry of Health** website (ⓦ www.sanita.it) also has pages on disabled facilities, including electric mobility scooters.

TOURIST INFORMATION

The **Italian Tourist Board ENIT** (ⓦ www.enit.it) will send out information packs if you tell them which areas you plan to

ADDRESSES

Genoa has two systems of street numbering which run alongside one another and seem to bear no relation to one another. Shops, businesses and some restaurants have one set of numbers, marked in red at their entrance and written with a lower case r in the address, while residences have black numbers.

visit. **Azienda di Promozione Turistica Genova (APT)** is the city's tourist agency, and is quite remarkably helpful. Its website (ⓦ www.apt.genova.it) is kept up to date and has lots of good links. There are tourist offices around the city, which have excellent maps and multilingual assistants. Opening hours are 09.30–13.00, 14.30–18.00:

Aeroporto Cristoforo Colombo ⓣ 010 6015247
Stazione Ferroviaria Principe ⓐ Piazza Acquaverde ⓣ 010 2462633
Smaller information points are at Piazza Matteotti and Porto Antico.

BACKGROUND READING

Desiring Italy by Susan Cahill. A collection of writings about Italy by women.

Numbers in the Dark by Italo Calvino (translated by Tim Parks). A collection of stories based in northern Italy.

The Silver Spoon, ed Linda Doesser. A doorstep of a book with a recipe for everything you've tried in Genoa and much, much more.

Bringing Italy Home and *La Dolce Vita* both by Ursula Ferrigno. Very accessible Italian recipes, including lots of treats from Liguria.

Emergencies

EMERGENCY NUMBERS

Emergency calls can be made from any telephone free of charge.

Ambulance (*Emergenza Sanitaria*) 🛈 118
Fire (*Vigili del Fuoco*) 🛈 115
Police (*carabinieri*) 🛈 112
Sea rescue 🛈 1530
Car breakdown 🛈 803 116 (connects to Automobile Club d'Italia)
Highway rescue 🛈 116

Lost or stolen credit cards
American Express 🛈 06 7 22 82
Diners Club 🛈 800 86 40 64
MasterCard 🛈 800 87 08 66
Visa 🛈 800 87 72 32

HOSPITALS

The standard of healthcare in Italy is reassuringly high.
Accident and Emergency departments are open 24 hours,
or you can call 🛈 118. This number will also provide you with
the address and contact number of doctors on emergency
call service. Many – but not all – of these doctors will speak
good English. The following hospitals in the city have
A&E departments:

Ospedale Galliera 🅰 Mura delle Cappucine 14 🛈 010 56231
Ospedale San Martino 🅰 Largo Rosanna Benzi 10 🛈 010 5551

EMERGENCY PHRASES

Help!	**Fire!**	**Stop!**
Aiuto!	Al fuoco!	Ferma!
Ahyootaw!	*Ahl fooawcaw!*	*Fairmah!*

Call an ambulance/a doctor/the police/the fire service!
Chiamate un'ambulanza/un medico/la polizia/i pompieri!
*Kyahmahteh oon ahmboolahntsa/oon mehdeecaw/
la pawleetsya/ee pompee-ehree!*

POLICE

In the event that you are mugged, pickpocketed or are the
victim of any kind of theft, you should contact the *carabinieri*
(these are the police whose uniform features black trousers
with a red stripe). You should do everything you legally can
to avoid being arrested in Genoa: Italy's laws concerning the
right to a lawyer and the number of hours you can be held
for questioning are not as liberal as those in Britain. Just to
illustrate the extent to which falling foul of the local legal
system can prolong a short city break, in Italy you can be held
for three years without trial.

The legal limit for blood alcohol while driving is 0.08 per
cent (0.25mg/l). Italian traffic police can and do carry out
random testing.

ACKNOWLEDGEMENTS
The publishers would like to thank the following individuals and organisations for supplying their copyright photographs for this book: Best Western Hotel Metropoli, page 39; Dreamstime (Bogdan, page 5; Davide Romanini, page 131); Echo Art, page 15; Flavio Ferrari, page 21; iStockphoto (lubilub, page 80; franco fojanini, page 102; lorenzo villavecchia, page 123; peeterv, page 127); Jan Fusco, pages 30, 37, 42 & 63); Dave Minogue, page 74; Pictures Colour Library, pages 7, 32, 44, 65, 82 & 105; Sferagrafica.com, page 96; World Pictures, pages 9, 19, 23, 25, 59 & 115; Pat Levy, all others.

Project Editor: Jennifer Jahn
Copy editor: Paul Hines
Proofreaders: Jan McCann & Cath Senker
Layout: Paul Queripel

Send your thoughts to
books@thomascook.com

- Found a great bar, club, shop or must-see sight that we don't feature?

- Like to tip us off about any information that needs a little updating?

- Want to tell us what you love about this handy little guidebook and more importantly how we can make it even handier?

Then here's your chance to tell all! Send us ideas, discoveries and recommendations today and then look out for your valuable input in the next edition of this title.

Email the above address (stating the title) or write to:
pocket guides Series Editor, Thomas Cook Publishing, PO Box 227, Coningsby Road, Peterborough PE3 8SB, UK.

WHAT'S IN YOUR GUIDEBOOK?

Independent authors Impartial up-to-date information from our travel experts who meticulously source local knowledge.

Experience Thomas Cook's 165 years in the travel industry and guidebook publishing enriches every word with expertise you can trust.

Travel know-how Thomas Cook has thousands of staff working around the globe, all living and breathing travel.

Editors Travel-publishing professionals, pulling everything together to craft a perfect blend of words, pictures, maps and design.

You, the traveller We deliver a practical, no-nonsense approach to information, geared to how you really use it.

Useful phrases

English	Italian	*Approx pronunciation*
BASICS		
Yes	Sì	*See*
No	No	*Noh*
Please	Per favore	*Pehr fahvohreh*
Thank you	Grazie	*Grahtsyeh*
Hello	Buongiorno/Ciao	*Bwonjohrnoh/Chow*
Goodbye	Arrivederci/Ciao	*Ahreevehderchee/Chow*
Excuse me	Scusi	*Skoozee*
Sorry	Mi dispiace	*Mee deespyahcheh*
That's okay	Va bene	*Vah behneh*
I don't speak Italian	Non parlo italiano	*Non pahrloh eetahlyahnoh*
Do you speak English?	Parla inglese?	*Pahrlah eenglehzeh?*
Good morning	Buongiorno	*Bwonjohrnoh*
Good afternoon	Buon pomeriggio	*Bwon pohmehreejoh*
Good evening	Buona sera	*Bwonah sehrah*
Goodnight	Buona notte	*Bwonah nohteh*
My name is ...	Mi chiamo ...	*Mee kyahmoh ...*
NUMBERS		
One	Uno	*Oonoh*
Two	Due	*Dooeh*
Three	Tre	*Treh*
Four	Quattro	*Kwahttroh*
Five	Cinque	*Cheenkweh*
Six	Sei	*Say*
Seven	Sette	*Sehteh*
Eight	Otto	*Ohtoh*
Nine	Nove	*Nohveh*
Ten	Dieci	*Dyehchee*
Twenty	Venti	*Ventee*
Fifty	Cinquanta	*Cheenkwahntah*
One hundred	Cento	*Chentoh*
SIGNS & NOTICES		
Airport	Aeroporto	*Ahehrohpohrtoh*
Railway station	Stazione ferroviaria	*Statsyoneh fehrohveeaahreeyah*
Platform	Binario	*Beenahreeyoh*
Smoking/non-smoking	Fumatori/non fumatori	*Foomahtohree/non foomahtohree*
Toilets	Bagni	*Bahnyee*
Ladies/Gentlemen	Signore/Signori	*Seenyoreh/Seenyohree*
Subway	Metropolitana	*Mehtrohpohleetahnah*